THE STATE OF THE ECONOMY
1992

THE STATE
OF THE ECONOMY
1992

Giles Keating · Peter Warburton

Walter Eltis · Douglas Fraser · John Ip

Mark Boléat · David A. Coleman

Alan Evans · Patrick Minford

David Lomax · Andrew Britton

Geoffrey Wood · David B. Coleman

Introduced by Colin Robinson

IEA
Institute of Economic Affairs
1992

First published in March 1992
by
THE INSTITUTE OF ECONOMIC AFFAIRS
2 Lord North Street, Westminster, London SW1P 3LB

IEA Readings 37

ISSN 0305-814X
ISBN 0-255 36304-4 (paper)

The Institute gratefully acknowledges financial support for its publications programme and other work from a generous benefaction by the late Alec and Beryl Warren.

Printed in Great Britain by
Goron Pro-Print Co. Ltd., Lancing, W. Sussex

Filmset in 'Berthold' Times Roman 11 on 12 point

CONTENTS

INTRODUCTION

Colin Robinson

Professor of Economics,
University of Surrey,
and Editorial Director,
Institute of Economic Affairs

MACRO-ECONOMIC FORECASTING is a difficult business. Like all forecasters, those who try to predict macro-economic events (especially in an open economy such as Britain's) are significantly in error most of the time. But since their predictions attract considerable public interest around actual or supposed turning points in the economy, their failings tend to be exposed sooner and with more publicity than those of forecasters concerned with particular industries.

The past year has been a particularly bad time for macro-economic forecasters, many of whom seriously under-estimated the depth of the downturn. All forecasters must analyse and interpret the past, since it is the principal guide to what may happen in the future. Yet the guidance it provides is extremely imperfect. The course of the present recession has demonstrated the problems of trying to predict by analogy with past recessions when a long period of growth and structural change in the economy has intervened. History has proved an even more imperfect guide than usual, principally because of the difficulty of incorporating in economic models the generally beneficial supply-side changes—and particularly the financial deregulation—of the 1980s. The behaviour of consumers and investors has been hard to predict in this first recession under the new régime.

No matter how chastening their recent experience, economic

forecasters can make progress only by learning from that experience—trying to understand why they made errors in the past, adapting their methods and making new forecasts which can again be tested against events. Moreover, it is a necessary (though not sufficient) condition for avoiding the grosser errors of economic policy that forecasting ability is improved so that policy-makers can estimate, if only roughly, the effects of maintaining current policies as compared with the effects of making changes.

The Institute of Economic Affairs therefore convenes each year a group of leading economic forecasters and others prominent in various fields of economic policy to express their views on the state of the economy and to indicate likely future developments. The January 1992 conference, revised versions of the papers from which appear in this volume, includes views on the economy in general and on some crucial sectors (the housing and labour markets and engineering), together with two papers on the European Monetary System. No one will be surprised, at the present juncture, to find a diversity of opinions both about the short-term outlook on an unchanged policy assumption and about the policy measures which might be appropriate both for the economy as a whole and for individual sectors.

In the first paper, *Giles Keating* makes a plea for lower interest rates. He points out that the easing in monetary policy has so far been limited because the banks have been widening their margins to compensate for increasing bad debts. Banks are also concerned about the adequacy of their capital relative to their loan books; consequently, their cautious attitude to lending may constrain economic recovery. He argues that the best way to help the banks and to promote recovery is to cut short-term rates to around $7\frac{1}{2}$ per cent by the end of 1992.

The unfortunate economic effects of political uncertainty because of the long-anticipated General Election (a point stressed by Keating) is taken up by *Peter Warburton* in the second paper; he also emphasises the difficulty of forecasting consumer and business responses to the unprecedented accumulation of debt in recent years. Warburton is concerned at the high level of real interest rates, recommending an immediate 2 percentage point cut in nominal rates, accompanied by the re-floating of sterling and measures to help small business if a year of zero or negative growth is to be avoided.

David Lomax's view is rather different. He argues that the present exchange rate relative to other European currencies allows British exports to compete but he is concerned about the effect on those exports of a world-wide slowdown in demand. Nevertheless, he expects 1·3 per cent real GDP growth in Britain in 1992, with a growth rate approaching that in the rest of Europe over the next five years. Lomax stresses the deterrent effect on business investment of periods of high inflation and wants to see government aim for a stable, low-inflation environment, at the same time stimulating investment in education and training and in infrastructure.

In view of the remarkable change in the housing market in the last few years and the macro-economic impact of that change, three papers are devoted to housing. *Mark Boléat* explains the reasons for the boom in the housing market and its subsequent very sharp decline in 1990 and 1991, when both the number of transactions and prices fell substantially (though with considerable regional variations). He expects only a modest recovery in 1992, given the large stock of unsold houses, the likely new supply in 1992 and the probable weak state of demand (attributable to fears about unemployment and higher personal taxation, and uncertainty about whether housing will be a good investment in future, all of which have depressed house prices). The package of measures to help home-owners announced in December 1991 will, he believes, have a marginally beneficial effect on housing market activity.

Alan Evans considers the costs of the British system of town and country planning which reduces the elasticity of the supply of housing with respect to price and, in conjunction with fiscal measures to encourage home ownership, leads both to a long-run upward trend in house prices and to considerable fluctuations in those prices. Thus the housing market is distorted and there are spillover effects in the rest of the economy. Home ownership is encouraged at the expense of the private rented sector, leading to a reduction in mobility; non-housing investment is reduced; wage demands may be stimulated; and the price of urban land is higher in Britain than in other European countries with less restrictive planning régimes.

David A. Coleman identifies the same reasons for the upward trend in house prices as does Evans. He considers the future of the private rented sector (smaller in Britain than in any other industrial country), pointing out the advantages of renting to the mobile job seeker. He concludes that there has been an extraordinary increase in new tenancies under the 1988 Housing Act and foresees a bright future for the private rented sector, provided there are some policy changes— such as a replacement for the Business Expansion Scheme (BES), extending tax advantages to institutions providing rented housing, and allowing the Housing Corporation to give grants to private sector institutions as well as to Housing Associations. Another suggestion is that more savers should be involved, perhaps through a housing TESSA.

In his discussion of the labour market, *Patrick Minford* argues that, in general, the Government has resisted the temptation to bail out ailing organisations and individuals during the present recession: thus the efficiency gains of the 1980s should not be lost. There has been a revolution in industrial relations: strikes are almost a thing of the past, unions are willing to co-operate with management in single-union plant deals, and wage bargaining has moved to the local from the national level. Union density has fallen to perhaps only 28 per cent in the private sector. The 'natural rate' of unemployment is, he estimates, only about 1 million. Output and employment could, with appropriate demand management, be about 5 per cent higher than they are now without stimulating excess demand.

Walter Eltis, Douglas Fraser and *John Ip* examine the engineering sector, which accounts for about 40 per cent of British manufacturing output, emphasising the differences between the successful sub-sectors—such as aerospace, electrical engineering and (recently) motor vehicles—and poor-performing industries such as mechanical engineering and metal goods. Both aerospace and capital plant manufacture now face problems, however, the former because of declining Ministry of Defence spending and the latter because protection of home suppliers is more difficult since most large utilities have been privatised and there are European rules on public procurement. The authors examine in some detail the influence of Japanese investment and Japanese methods on the automotive industry, the sector of engineering which has most improved its performance in recent years. They also examine skills shortages and imperfect management training in engineering, and apparent links to inadequate rewards. They argue against devaluation and lower interest rates as 'solutions' to British industry's problems. Instead, they want a long period of sustainable growth in the economy during which the lessons learned by the motor industry—in adopting Japanese and other best practices—can be applied to the rest of British industry.

Given the importance of the existing European Monetary System (EMS) and the prospective European Monetary Union (EMU), it is fitting that this volume ends with two papers on these subjects.

Geoffrey Wood and *David B. Coleman* contend that the EMU Treaty has not been well designed. In their view, there are practical reasons (because of nominal wage inertia and long-term contracts in nominal terms) why there should be inflation convergence before monetary union; however, the fiscal convergence requirements may be harmful. They raise some awkward questions about how the European Central Bank, in pursuing the desirable aim of price stability (which they suggest should mean a 0-2 per cent per annum price trend), will be able to determine the required initial money stock and what index should be used to measure whether or not prices are stable. They also question whether the proposed relationship between the European Central Bank (responsible for monetary policy) and the Council of Finance Ministers (responsible for exchange rate policy) is workable.

Andrew Britton also points out that there is no definition of the price stability aim; he expects European central bankers to aim for an inflation rate no lower than Germany has achieved in the last decade (2-3 per cent a year on average). Britton stresses the technical problems which the new central banking system will face and anticipates greater instability of output growth than in the 1980s. He argues against a small devaluation of sterling now which would have little effect on competitiveness but would demonstrate a weak commitment to a fixed exchange rate. Nevertheless, he is concerned about finding alternatives to devaluation for regions which find unemployment mounting. Flexible wages and prices would help to correct imbalances but he would also like to see modifications to tax and expenditure systems designed to increase their ability to act as automatic stabilisers.

The Institute of Economic Affairs is delighted to publish this book, with its stimulating collection of views on the economic outlook and economic policy, as a contribution to the debate on the future of the British economy within Europe. The views expressed are, of course, those of the authors and not those of the Institute (which has no corporate view), its Trustees, its Directors or its Advisers.

February 1992   COLIN ROBINSON

THE BRITISH ECONOMY: SUSTAINED RECOVERY DEPENDS ON LOW INTEREST RATES

Giles Keating

Chief Economist,
Credit Suisse First Boston

Summary and Introduction

THE MAIN MESSAGE of this paper is that the UK will see a sustainable recovery starting in 1992 only if interest rates fall sharply, maybe even towards 7½ per cent by the end of the year. The reason why low interest rates are so important is because the banks are weak and this weakness is one of the key factors preventing economic recovery. Obviously the world environment is not favourable either but among domestic causes, this is possibly the most crucial. Banking weakness will continue, delaying and dampening the recovery, unless interest rates fall sharply. The other key message of this paper is that a large fall in UK interest rates does not mean that sterling has to leave the Exchange Rate Mechanism (ERM) or devalue within it. This theme is addressed towards the end of the paper.

The paper begins by examining the state of the UK banking system, to see why it is in trouble, what the effects of its difficulties are, and also to explain how lower interest rates go to the heart of that problem.

The macro-economic statistics give some indication of what is going on. The figures show a marked fall in personal sector credit in the three months to November 1991; the aggregate bank and building society lending counterpart to M4 grew at only 4·6 per cent annualised over the

Chart 1: UK Clearing Banks: Ratio of Bad Debts to Advances, 1980-91

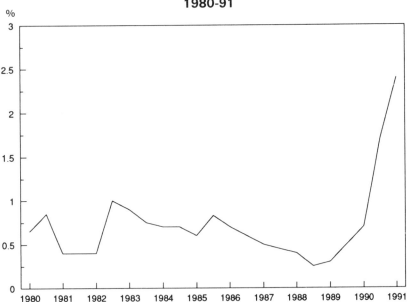

most recent three months, an extremely low figure by recent standards. Moreover, a large part of that is due to interest crediting and so that growth figure implies effective credit expansion close to zero if interest crediting is removed.

Worrying Rise in Loan Losses

The micro-economic information on the experiences of the individual banks shows a picture that is possibly more worrying. The TSB has just reported a loss, the Midland and NatWest are likely to follow suit. Between them, the major UK banks are expected to report provisions against bad debts of some £6·5 billion for 1991. For the TSB, loan losses are now estimated at 3·5 per cent of the outstanding loan book. So out of every £100 they have lent, at the moment they are losing £3·50. Other banks also have very high loan losses, and these have been rising sharply (see Chart 1).

Let us look behind these figures for a moment and see why it is that the loan losses have been going up so sharply. It is essentially for two reasons. One is the costs of servicing loans, relative to the ability to meet those costs. That has clearly worsened substantially, partly because interest rates, although well down from their peak, are still very high. (One of the themes that I will develop shortly is that the fall in base rates, from 15 per cent down to 10½ per cent, exaggerates the decline in loan servicing costs faced by anybody with a variable rate loan, particularly small commercial borrowers.) While interest charges remain high, income has been squeezed, particularly for many corporate borrowers. So, servicing difficulties are a reason for the increase in defaults.

Another problem is the collapse in collateral values, as asset prices have fallen, in particular real estate prices of one sort or another. To illustrate the collapse in collateral prices I have had to use some housing market data, because the data that we have on the banking sector is limited. Perhaps the CSO will improve this situation. Chart 2 shows that although house prices in the UK as a whole have only fallen by one or two per cent since the boom, in some of the individual regions the losses have been horrendous. The worst loss of all by region was in East Anglia where prices are down by 35 per cent from the peak. So somebody who was unfortunate enough to buy, say, an average house in East Anglia at the end of 1988 paid £100,000 for it. They now have an asset worth £65,000; so they are £35,000 into the red and obviously, whoever lent to them (with, let us say, an 80 per cent mortgage) now has collateral worth £15,000 less than the value of the outstanding debt. Repossessions have risen dramatically and defaults are following.

Impact of Rising Defaults on the Banks

Turning back to the banks, what is the impact of rising defaults? One effect is that there is clearly a worsening in the credit quality of their customers. The average probability of any given customer reneging on his debt has gone up. The other effect is that bank capital is eroded. Within a bank balance sheet, capital provides a kind of cushion to protect deposits from any bad experience on loans. A bank is in the business of taking deposits in and lending them out again, and in good times, if it makes a profit on the loans, then that has a leveraged effect, giving it a high rate of return on its capital. Conversely, in bad times, if a bank makes losses on its loans, then it is the capital that gets squeezed very heavily, while depositors are not affected, unless the losses are so extreme that all the capital is wiped out.

The banks, throughout virtually the whole of the 1980s, had very healthy loan books; their losses, as a percentage of their total loan

3

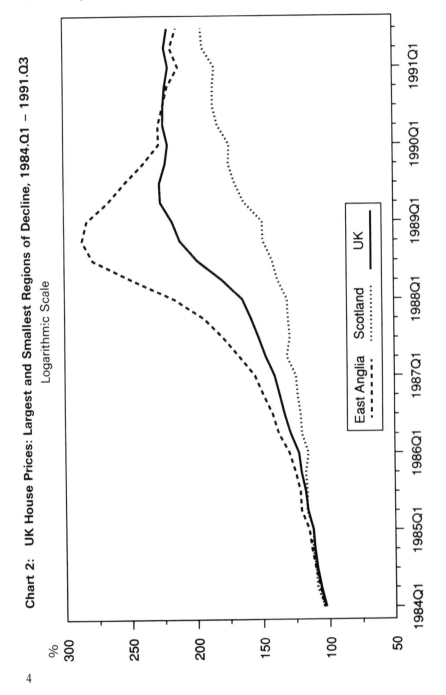

Chart 2: UK House Prices: Largest and Smallest Regions of Decline, 1984.Q1 – 1991.Q3

Logarithmic Scale

book, stood at about 0·5 per cent. With a spread between deposit and loan rates of 3 per cent or so (the exact figure varying with type of business and over time), and with net non-interest costs of about 1·5 per cent of loans, the banks were able to make a good profit. The situation now is much more difficult. Loan losses have risen extremely sharply, to around 1·5 per cent, which virtually wipes out the banks' profits (although reported figures are also affected by other factors, notably returns on foreign subsidiaries).

How do the banks respond to this worsening of their loss experience? One response is to push up their margins between deposit and loan rates. In the middle of last year there was a public debate about this, because as base rates came down, the interest paid on deposits came down sharply but the banks made much smaller reductions in the rates they charged on loans, particularly for small businesses. But the banks were attempting to make up for the big increase in defaults by widening their margins. As we saw in the case of the TSB, they did not do it enough, so they made losses.

This widening of margins means that the easing of monetary policy so far is much more limited than it looks. Only a rather small part of the cut in base rates has come through to benefit borrowers. But on the other hand, the rates paid to depositors have fallen roughly in line with base rates. So, as is typical in the early stages of a monetary easing, monetary policy is of very limited effectiveness, and for brief periods may even have a perverse effect. Nor do the banks' shareholders feel richer because of the widening spread; the shareholders feel poorer because of the losses.

Widening Margins of Banks and Building Societies

Unfortunately, it is not possible to obtain good figures on the widening of bank spreads. Data from the banks' reports are too opaque. However, there are reasonably good figures for the building societies. Chart 3 shows the difference between the average mortgage rate and the average rate paid on deposits. At the peak of the house price boom (July 1988) the spread was down almost to 3½ per cent. As the boom ended, the spread widened. So the building societies have managed to get a rise in margins.

One of the reasons why the banks and the building societies have been able to expand their margins is that, in some cases, their monopoly power increases during this recessionary phase. This is in stark contrast to the period of deregulation and credit expansion in the

Chart 3: Building Society Margins, August 1984 – August 1991

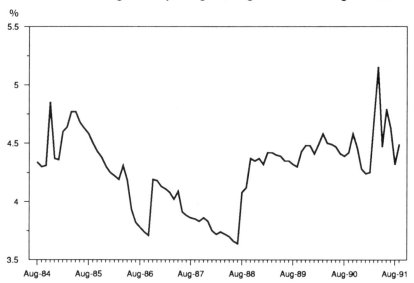

1980s, which saw margins being competed downwards. As the volume of bad debts has increased, so the monopoly power of the banks has also increased because customers can no longer shop around freely among banks. If there is any kind of question mark over their business at all, they are more or less going to be locked into their existing bank. Hence the banks have been able to expand margins; and hence economic performance at the moment is very different from the way that it was back in 1988. Late last year the Treasury announced that they were going to commission some outside economists to investigate the effect of credit deregulation on the economy, a classic example of forecasters bolting the stable door after the horse has bolted. That is not the issue at the moment.

Capital Adequacy Rules and Banks' Caution

The bank capital position is also an important consideration. UK banks are now subject to the Bank of England rules, which are in turn consistent with the rules agreed internationally through the Bank for International Settlements (BIS). These capital adequacy rules require the banks to have a certain amount of capital relative to their loan book. The precise details of how this is computed are not relevant here, but in outline the requirement is that banks must have equity or

TABLE 1

ESTIMATED YEAR-END 1991 BIS TIER 1 RATIOS

	%
Barclays	5·5
Lloyds	5·4
Midland	5·0/4·9
NatWest	5·0

equity-equivalent capital (called 'Tier 1') worth 4 per cent of their loan book, and total capital worth 8 per cent. These figures must be achieved, and in practice the banks will aim to have 5 per cent Tier 1 (see Table 1).

The Table shows estimated capital ratios for the big four UK clearing banks at the end of 1991. The Midland and NatWest in particular are at the informal target of 5 per cent for Tier 1 capital. In good times, this would matter very little, because the banks could either accumulate extra capital by retaining profits, or they could raise extra capital in the markets. Unfortunately that is not the position at the moment. For example, the Midland appears to be running at a loss and yet it paid out an interim dividend, so it has been running down its capital. Moreover, the Chairman of one of the clearers was sufficiently worried to have asked the Bank of England for the BIS ratios to be relaxed last year, and although his request was rejected, his concern was clearly shown by that action.

So capital adequacy is at least a potential problem. At the least, it re-inforces the cautious approach to lending which the banks are already adopting as a result of the rise in defaults. This caution is already evident in the macro-economic data for bank lending in late 1991. For 1992, the banks will not want to expand their loan books by more than a very small amount, perhaps 4 to 5 per cent. For a recovery, nominal GDP would have to grow by at least 7 per cent, and bank lending usually grows faster than GDP in a recovery to finance rising inventories. This leads to the conclusion that economic recovery in the UK is not so much going to be braked by the position of the banks, as virtually to be halted by it (see Chart 4).

The Bank of England argues that this is not an important problem, because big companies can ignore the banks and access the capital

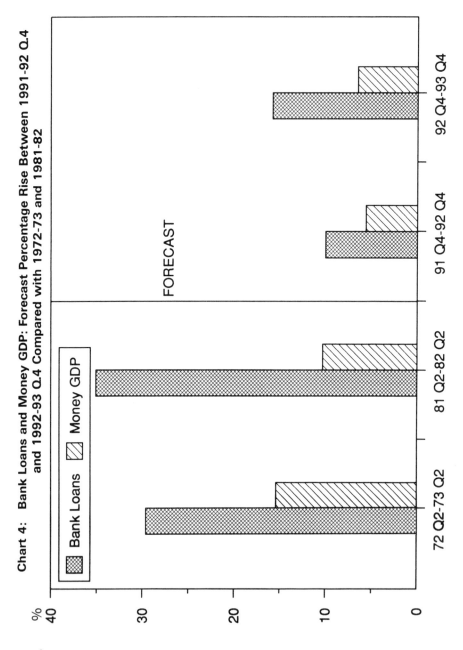

Chart 4: Bank Loans and Money GDP: Forecast Percentage Rise Between 1991-92 Q.4 and 1992-93 Q.4 Compared with 1972-73 and 1981-82

markets directly. This argument can be turned on its head; arguably, this is a disaster because it means that the banks tend to lose their best customers and are left with the rump which is likely to have the worst loan experience. This worsens the banks' profitability and increases their caution.

Policy Solutions

How should the Government confront this problem? Fortunately, the UK is nowhere near the situation facing the Norwegian government last year, which had to nationalise the whole of the country's bankrupt banking system. For the UK, relaxing the BIS capital adequacy ratios is one possibility. The trouble is that this could send a bad signal to the markets, implying that the banks are in worse shape than they are, thus making it even more difficult for the banks to raise extra capital; it could even create a sense of panic in the country. So this is not advisable, although a discreet easing of some of the detailed rules is a possibility.

Another approach is to reduce the banks' reserve ratios at the central bank. The reserve ratios are in effect a tax on the banks since they carry a zero or below-market rate of interest. In the UK, the scope to do this is limited, because the reserve ratios are already very small; nevertheless, the Bank of England has made two minor reductions since the start of 1991, the latest effective from 31 January 1992 and saving the banks about £20 million. Interestingly, other countries—the United States just over a year ago and France much more recently—have adopted exactly this tactic. Another possibility would be to reduce explicitly the tax on banks, but this is unlikely to prove politically popular and would not help loss-making banks.

The remaining way of helping the banks is to reduce short-term interest rates further. This may result in a further expansion of the banks' margins, so that the rates the banks charge their borrowers do not come down as much as base rates. Although this means that the immediate impact of lower base rates on the economy is dampened, it is nevertheless good over a slightly longer period because it restores bank profitability and breaks open the credit log-jam described above. So lower short-term rates are really the key, and as suggested at the beginning of this paper, possibly rates even as low as 7·5 per cent or somewhere towards that level could be appropriate.

Future Path for Sterling

Does this mean that sterling has to leave the ERM, or be devalued within it? Probably not. Devaluation would be likely to destroy credibility and would undermine the downward pressure on wages that we have been seeing; it could even have a perverse effect, causing upward pressure on interest rates, because it would undermine perceptions of the Government's commitment to the ERM. Leaving the ERM would allow the currency to fall to a low enough level for short rates to decline substantially, but such a move would have an air of crisis about it which could have a counter-productive impact on overall confidence in the economy. So neither devaluation nor leaving the ERM is an attractive option.

What is the alternative? The main reason why the ERM is preventing lower UK interest rates is that the markets are demanding a risk premium to reflect political uncertainty. What needs to happen is for the political uncertainty to be removed by having the General Election as soon as possible. This is not a political recommendation but rather a comment about managing the economy, and particularly about tackling the banking problem identified here. Once the election is out of the way, then we have the scope for interest rates to come down. Under a Tory government probably this could happen really very easily, under a Labour government it could be more difficult, but Labour has one very easy way to achieve this objective, which would be a logical counterpart to that party's endorsement of monetary union. This would be to announce that the Bank of England is going to be made independent. The credibility gained from that should have the beneficial effect on interest rates that is required.

Can low UK interest rates, perhaps close to 7·5 per cent, be consistent with the German Lombard rate at 9·75 and German money market rates at around 9·5 per cent? Two points are relevant. One is that the German wages situation has now reached a crisis point and it looks as though that is going to result in wage rises not very far from where the Bundesbank wants them, that is, at around 5·5 per cent, allowing the Bundesbank to move to cutting short-term rates, perhaps in the second quarter of this year. That would be helpful.

The other point is that after the election, and possibly with an independent central bank, there is no reason why UK interest rates should not come down below German rates. Why should that be possible for Britain, when for France there have been only short periods when rates have been below German levels, and then by only a narrow margin? The answer is that Britain still has the big advantage of the broad ERM band and it also has the advantage that both major political parties claim that they are committed to entering the narrow band at the current parity of DM2·95. So in mechanical terms there is no reason, if sterling is, say, at 2·85 against the Deutschemark, why the market should not be anticipating over the next year or so that sterling with virtual certainty is going to rise up towards that 2·95 central parity and then join the narrow band. That expectation of an appreciation would compensate investors for sterling rates being significantly below German rates. So with the credibility of either a re-elected Tory government, or a Labour government announcing an independent central bank, that would be a possible outcome and, indeed, would be the desirable and perhaps the only one for the economy, resolving the bank problem addressed in this paper.

2

FLOAT STERLING, CUT INTEREST RATES

Peter Warburton
Robert Fleming Securities Limited

Introduction

FORECASTING is always a very hazardous occupation. One can identify the economists in any gathering who are involved in forecasting as those with thick dotted lines around their necks bearing the inscription 'cut here'. I am particularly aware of the hazard, having challenged the prevailing orthodoxy in the context of a letter to *The Times* last week.[1] When John Major refers to 'dismal Jimmies' I suppose I have to regard myself as being included in that, since my middle name is James. (Incidentally, it was 'Jimmies' that he said and *not* 'Johnnies' which would have reflected rather more on himself!)

This paper presents some UK economic forecasts, summarised in Table 1, based upon a non-consensus view of domestic policy constraints and external factors. However, the consensus (in terms of 1992 growth expectations) has been slipping from about last October onwards. Our controversial view of inflation prospects draws a distinction between internationally traded and domestic sectors of the

---

[1] 'Clearing obstacles to economic and monetary recovery', Letters to the Editor, *The Times*, 7 January 1992. The letter was signed by Professor Tim Congdon, Bill Martin, Professor Patrick Minford, Professor Gordon Pepper, Professor Sir Alan Walters, and Peter Warburton.

TABLE 1

ECONOMIC OVERVIEW OF 1992 AND 1993

Annual percentage change	1989	1990	1991E[1]	1992F[2]	1993F[2]
Economic growth	2·2	1·0	−2·5	0·0	1·3
Consumer spending	3·5	1·0	−1·6	−1·2	1·0
Fixed investment	6·8	−2·2	−11·1	−5·8	4·3
Inflation (GDP measure)	7·4	8·4	6·5	5·3	5·7
Inflation (RPI measure)	7·8	9·5	5·9	5·5	6·5
Visible trade balance (£bn.)	−24·6	−18·7	−10·0	−12·5	−8·5
Current balance (£bn.)	−20·4	−14·4	−6·0	−8·0	−5·0
PSBR (Fin. yr. £bn.)	−7·9	−0·5	11·5	21·0	32·0
Average earnings (whole economy)	9·1	9·7	8·0	6·2	5·5
Unemployment (million)	1·8	1·7	2·3	2·8	3·1

[1] E = Estimated.   [2] F = Forecast.

economy. Finally, some controversial remedies for our current dilemma are proposed.

Background to the Forecast

The policy background to the forecasts took a decisive change of course more than a year ago when sterling entered the Exchange Rate Mechanism (ERM). John Major's strategy was designed to break the inflationary mentality in the UK. Despite the onset of recession, John Major and Norman Lamont embarked on an exercise in brinkmanship and it was a very risky strategy. The expectation was that joining the ERM would not only have a deflationary impact on pay settlements in the traded goods sector, the manufacturing sector, but would have a pervasive effect on wage settlements in the whole economy. This strategy was dependent for its success on securing a fall in underlying inflation rather greater than has, in fact, occurred. The expectation was that by now the UK economy would be sitting pretty. The exchange rate would be at or above its ERM central parity, exerting downward pressure on inflation expectations; the economy would be moving comfortably out of recession. It is necessary to understand why that is not the case in order to examine what is likely to happen in the coming year.

A decisive point for our own forecast came during October 1991 when the November election option was closed off. Until then, our projection was for 1 per cent economic growth this year. The delayed election, and necessarily delayed base-rate cuts, prompted us to reduce our forecast to one of zero growth. Zero is a central forecast and that must be emphasised. Neither 2 per cent real growth, which is still something like the Government's forecast, nor a 2 per cent contraction of output are likely outcomes, but they are equally probable.

Because of the advanced stage of the political cycle and because of the problems of the financial and housing sectors, it is pointless to make a forecast which does not assume some policy reaction to these factors. If the Government were to agree that they were confronting a year of zero economic growth, it is certain that they would wish to do something about it. One might consider that an extension of existing policies might very well secure a poorer outcome than zero. That is the rather unpalatable conclusion to which our analysis and forecasts lead.

The wider than usual range of conceivable outcomes on economic growth stems from three sources of uncertainty. First, there is the interest rate and exchange rate uncertainty that has arisen because of the divergent trends of German (and therefore European) interest rates relative to US interest rates. It is very clear that having a banking system with the same kind of problems as the USA (and, indeed, Japan and Canada as well) would make the US, and indeed the Japanese, trend in short-term interest rates much more appropriate to our own situation than that of German rates, which has been upwards. Inseparable from the interest rate uncertainty is obviously the exchange rate uncertainty. The forward exchange market, three years out, is discounting a devaluation of sterling. It is indicative that even the forward rate reflects an expectation that sterling cannot hold its existing parity.

Secondly, there is still great uncertainty over the result of the General Election. Far be it for an economist to blacken the character of any particular group of politicians, but it would have been very beneficial for the economy had the election been held last year. Many economic decisions have been postponed or diluted as a result of this delay and the sooner this election is out of the way the better.

Thirdly, there is the unpredictability of business and consumer responses to the excessive accumulation of debt. It is important to distinguish two views of what is going on since, to some extent, we are in unknown territory. What has happened over the last 10 years in a number of countries, but notably not Germany, is that the household liabilities to income ratio has risen markedly. In the UK, an increase in liabilities from about 50 per cent of annual disposable income to about 100 per cent has occurred. The Treasury view is that, once the debt to income ratio has stabilised and income gearing (that is, the burden of interest payments as a percentage of income) has fallen back, then consumer spending will resume its growth at the same pace as previously, something around 2-3 per cent per annum. There is an alternative view that some reduction in this debt/income ratio will be required, as well as a reduction in income gearing, before it would be prudent to talk about a resumption of normal growth of personal consumption. The support for this view derives from a number of economic relationships in which a period of overshooting occurs, of what comes to be regarded as the new equilibrium of economic behaviour. The phenomenon of 'de-leveraging' is well known to Americans and will soon be evident in the UK. This observation gives another clue to the source of our caution.

Forecast Details and Underlying Assumptions

This leads on to the composition of economic growth in the UK economy. On consumer spending, a further contraction of real consumer spending this year of slightly more than 1 per cent is expected. Our estimate of the fall last year was 1·6 per cent.

Fixed investment is a curate's egg. There is likely to be an improvement in housing and in some areas of business investment this year. But, clearly, in commercial buildings, leased assets and various other categories there will probably be further declines. NEDO construction output forecasts are extremely downbeat for 1992.

Stockbuilding represents a big area of uncertainty. The surprising thing about this recession has been that de-stocking, which normally occurs early in a recession, was concentrated in the first half of last year when recession was well under way. Because of the penal level of real interest rates, the carrying cost of stocks will remain high and will obstruct a strong inventory rebound in 1992. Nevertheless, stocks were such a negative influence on growth last year that the year-to-year effect can only be positive.

Nor are we able to share the prevailing optimism about world trade growth this year, and therefore UK export volumes. Looking at the *OECD Economic Outlook* document published in December, it seems to represent an aggregation of the unrealistic ambitions of individual countries. Each is hopeful of an antidote to weak domestic demand. To forecast 2·2 per cent growth for the G7 nations and 5·5 per cent growth in the exports of those same countries, goes against the tenor of international trade relations at a time when the important Uruguay talks are seemingly on the verge of collapse. Our forecast assumes world trade growth of something closer to 2 per cent in 1992, similar to the growth which is likely to be recorded for last year. This obviously limits the scope for export performance not only by the UK but also by Germany, where strong hopes of an export rebound were held following the pre-occupation with satisfying domestic demand last year.

Without specifying precisely how this might occur, it is assumed that UK base rates will fall to 8 per cent by the third quarter, but with a possible increase towards the end of the year as the first signs of recovery emerge. The government would clearly not want to run the risk of over-stimulating demand and triggering a new cycle of inflation.

German short-term interest rates are critical to this assumption. We assume no change in rates until the start of the second half of the year when, from their current 9·4 per cent, money market rates will move towards 8 per cent by the end of the year. US banks' prime rate is assumed to fall only slightly from the current 6·5 per cent to 6 per cent, drifting back towards 7 per cent by the end of 1992.

Again, without describing at this stage how it will come about, we expect sterling to finish 1992 with a parity of DM2·65 rather than the current DM2·84 and central parity of DM2·95. The assumptions about fiscal policy are problematic, but the general drift is going to be towards a more relaxed fiscal policy. Certainly, once privatisation proceeds diminish or cease altogether this will expose higher underlying deficits, which are expected over the next couple of years to reach perhaps 4 or 5 per cent of nominal GDP. The European influence will be to re-inforce the tendency towards a relaxation of fiscal policy as a counter-balance to the tight money discipline inherent at the moment in the ERM. Thus, we present a very cautious picture of economic growth in 1992, with no guarantee of strong recovery in 1993. This caution is founded on three propositions and this is probably where, at some point, almost everybody will disagree with the analysis.

o Real UK interest rates, however defined, are inappropriately high in relation not only to the current rate of economic growth but also to the long-run sustainable rate of economic growth.

o Sterling is over-valued in the Exchange Rate Mechanism and also, in fact more so, in relation to the US dollar and the Japanese yen.

o UK labour market adjustment continues to operate principally on the level of employment rather than through the moderation of pay inflation, despite the beneficial reforms of the 1980s. (That is a very important qualifying phrase.)

High Real Interest Rates

First of all, it is contended that the continuation of high real interest rates (which is a central element of UK economic policy) is mistaken. Excessive real interest rates prior to and during a period of output recession destroy economic capacity, strengthen oligopolies and monopolies and limit the future pace of economic growth. For the Government, there appears to be no perceived inconsistency in maintaining real interest rates of at least 3 or 4 per cent and even of 5 or 6 per cent. The Chancellor has never given any clues that he would regard economic growth or economic recovery as being hindered or prevented by prospective real interest rates at this level. And here, of course, we imply the use of retail prices. Using manufacturing producer prices, even greater real interest rates result. Using asset prices, which are falling, implies huge real interest rates. How do we know that real interest rates are excessive? I suggest six indications:

1. *Because the demand for new borrowing by the financially sound has fallen.* (Of course, the great majority of all borrowers are financially sound—that must be emphasised.) Private sector credit growth has fallen from an annual rate of 24·7 per cent in late 1988 to 6·3 per cent on the most recent data. In other words, a severe contraction of the growth of new borrowing has taken place. Consumer credit outstanding (that is, bank overdrafts and other forms of credit), which was expanding annually by almost 14 per cent in 1989, is now growing by barely 3 per cent. The most expensive forms of borrowing, finance house credit and bank credit cards, show divergent trends. On the one hand, finance house credit is actually being repaid at a strenuous rate; on the other, bank credit card borrowing, which is more of a passive response, is the fastest growing of the elements of consumer credit.

2. *Because voluntary repayment of debt by consumers and companies has become more common.* Although numerically not very signifi-

cant, lump-sum voluntary repayments of building society mortgages alone increased by 53 per cent in the first nine months of 1991 over the first nine months of 1990. Companies, by virtue of their capital raising activities (principally in the equity market), have repaid a chunk of their bank loans. So we have moved from an increase in industrial and commercial companies' debt of £28 billion in 1989, to a repayment of about £300 million last year. And more recently, unincorporated businesses (small firms, partnerships, etc.) have also begun to make net repayments of bank debt.

3. *Because UK banks are scarcely profitable.* Following on from comments that Giles Keating made in his paper, the level of real profits of UK banks has plummeted. Using 1985 prices as a scaling factor, real profits slumped from nearly £4 billion in 1988 to £1·1 billion in 1990 and to, perhaps, almost zero in 1991. The implied rate of return on banks' equity was something like 30 per cent at the peak in 1988 and only 7 per cent in 1990. If the banks could identify profitable opportunities at these real interest rates, then this would not be happening.

4. *By contrasting real rates in the UK today with those during previous recessions and with real rates in other countries with similarly geared household and corporate sector balance sheets.* This assertion would take a long time to validate; more information is available to interested parties.

5. *From the incidence of debt delinquency and its composition.* A lot of publicity has been given to the house repossession mountain but little concerning the principal causes of repossession or the fact that a lot of the repossessions occur outside the building society sector. On our information, the three most common causes of house repossession are: first, dissolution of the household, comprising failed marriages and all other cases where loose associations of co-dwellers are terminated. Many home-buying co-operatives that were formed in 1988 have since broken up as former flatmates have left to pursue their own careers or to get married. So, dissolution of a household has a wider application than the failure of marriages. Secondly, failure of a business secured against the home. Building societies, as far as we are aware, do not collect data on this basis, but banks require personal collateral for small businesses in roughly 50 per cent of cases. It can be inferred that the scale of business failure

has helped to drive mortgage repossession to its current heights. Again, this is a side-effect of high real interest rates. Thirdly, as companies seek to conserve cash flow, job-shedding occurs, not only of the main but also of the second earner. When married women lose their jobs, often there is no recorded increase in unemployment. Yet this can have a material impact on the ability of a household to service the mortgage.

6. *Finally, from the weakness of demand for private housing and commercial property.*

Overvaluation of Sterling

An overvalued exchange rate is forcing down the profitability of producers operating solely from the UK. Multinationals are much better able to tolerate the pound at this level but are likely to minimise output from UK locations. How do we know that sterling is over-valued in the ERM?

1. In principle, because the foreign exchange market tells us so. Sterling, we contend, was only really comfortable in the ERM when the German Deutschemark (DM) was depreciating against the dollar and the yen. Between October 1991 and early January 1992, the DM has been appreciating against these currencies and sterling has lagged behind. Despite repeated affirmation of the policy commitment to the existing central parity by all main political parties, but most significantly by the Governor of the Bank of England and the Prime Minister, sterling fell to DM2·84 and to the bottom of the EMS. So, if the policy were credible, if people really believed that the pound would return to DM2·95, there would be a huge speculative demand in favour of sterling because of the limitation of downside risk. It is because people do not believe that the downside risk is limited in this way that sterling is not shooting back towards its central parity.

2. Because export profitability has been eroded since the UK joined the ERM, it is making life more difficult for the internationally exposed sector.

3. UK unit labour cost differentials have widened with Germany since ERM entry; that is largely because of the much earlier and deeper recession in this country and is now being corrected. But the UK started off very much on the wrong foot.

4. Because the volume of UK goods imports has fallen by only 5 per cent during this recession, so far, compared with 21 per cent in 1981 and 14 per cent in 1975. Within a flexible exchange rate régime, the currency has tended to weaken in recessions. Being in the ERM has prevented the repetition of this pattern and enabled foreign producers to retain market share and profitability in UK markets.

5. Because export volumes, of industries whose production is mostly sourced domestically, have performed poorly since we joined the ERM. Obviously, this is also conditional on how severely they have cut back in terms of their unit labour and material costs.

Real Wage Resistance

Real wage resistance throws too large a burden of adjustment in recession on to corporate profits. A period of zero or negative real wage growth (for those in work) is essential if UK corporate profitability is to narrow the gap with other members of the G7. Why has nominal wage inflation remained so stubbornly high in the midst of recession, business failure and unemployment?

1. The legacy of the Lawson boom is a disbelief of individuals and companies in government inflation forecasts. This is very sad. The Treasury used to have a very good inflation forecasting record and perhaps last year will help to repair that reputation in terms of the headline RPI. But the headline RPI overstates the underlying reduction in the rate of inflation. The general public cannot be criticised for doubting that inflation has really fallen as far as the Government maintains. This point can be illustrated (Chart 1) by dividing the retail price index into two roughly equal parts. In the first are included the prices over which the government exercises direct or indirect control or which have a high commodity content— that is, housing costs, rail fares, petrol, drink and tobacco prices. This category was the source of inflation reduction during 1991. The remaining category is private sector non-commodity prices. These were affected by the rise in the rate of VAT, which will drop out in April, but it is evident that there has been very little erosion of private sector inflation during the course of the past year. That is changing but I do not think it can change sufficiently rapidly to prevent an increase in the headline inflation rate to 5·5 per cent this year.

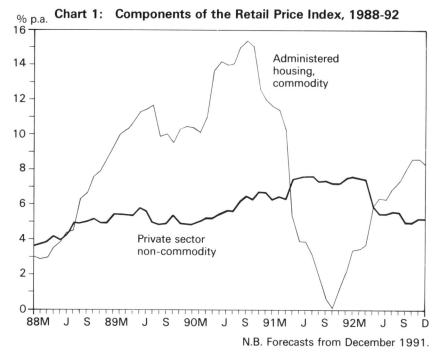

% p.a. **Chart 1: Components of the Retail Price Index, 1988-92**

N.B. Forecasts from December 1991.

2. Because companies were incorrectly advised, first, that there would be no recession, next, that the recession would be mild and brief, then that recovery was imminent. The lateness of destocking is evidence of the unpreparedness of businesses for the recession.

3. Because employers in the traded goods sector failed to appreciate or to capitalise on the strength of their bargaining position over pay in 1991. Even before ERM entry it should have been obvious that the extent of EC spare capacity had weakened the hand of their workforces.

4. Because too large a percentage of UK economic activity is protected from international competitive pressures. Inflation in the consumer services sector (ex-housing services) is still running at around 8 or 9 per cent. The deflator for government expenditure reached 9·2 per cent in the third quarter of 1991. Too high a proportion of UK employers have been able to afford 7 per cent-plus pay awards in the past 12 months.

Remedies

Given the forecasts and underlying analysis presented above, it is appropriate to conclude with some suggested remedies. The principal remedy is to cut interest rates by 2 percentage points (to 8·5 per cent) immediately. In practical terms it appears there is no other way to implement this than to float sterling and allow the currency to find its own level. This does not presume that sterling would actually depreciate by a huge amount. Arguably, there is no credibility in attempting to sustain a policy stance which is clearly so uncomfortable and inconsistent with domestic circumstances and problems. To drop this pretence of policy sustainability could actually enhance credibility. Sterling need not fall a great distance.

Since it is essential to replace the ERM discipline by something else, it is recommended that targets for broad money growth be re-instated and guidelines for acceptable private sector credit growth introduced as well. To facilitate the operation of monetary policy, the practice of fully funding the Public Sector Borrowing Requirement (PSBR) should be abandoned.

Given the way that companies have been penalised in this recession, some micro-economic measures are also in order. Uniform business rate should be frozen at its existing level for two years. Many more small businesses should be lifted out of the VAT registration net and a doubling of the VAT exemption limit from £35,000 to £70,000 is advocated. Finally, legislation to penalise and otherwise discourage late payment of invoices by large and medium-sized firms is overdue. The overall effect of implementing these remedies would make a big difference to the economic outlook and would take us closer to the, as yet, unlikely plus 2 per cent rate of growth and deliver us from the unacceptable minus 2 per cent.

THE ENGINEERING CHALLENGE

Walter Eltis

Director General

Douglas Fraser

Industrial Director

John Ip

Head of Industrial Economics,
National Economic Development Office

THE ENGINEERING INDUSTRY produces two-fifths of United Kingdom manufacturing output, so our prosperity rests on its prosperity. The distinction is often drawn between the chemical-based industries where the UK performs comparatively well, and the physics-based industries where our performance is weaker. This contrast is brought out in the tables and charts below.

The Performance of the United Kingdom Engineering Industry

Table 1 shows growth over the 1979-89 cycle. It will be evident that while GDP grew at an average annual rate of 2·2 per cent in these 10 years, manufacturing growth was only 1·2 per cent. Within the manufacturing total, the chemicals industries including pharmaceuticals grew at an average rate of 2·6 per cent, that is, somewhat faster than GDP, while engineering grew at only 0·8 per cent, considerably slower than the manufacturing total and less than one-third as fast as the chemicals sector. But the performance of engineering was by no means the weakest of the British manufacturing industries. The output of textiles and clothing actually fell at an annual rate of 1·6 per cent from 1979 to 1989.

TABLE 1

REAL GROWTH RATES IN THE UK, 1979-89

	Annual average real growth rates (1979-89)
Manufacturing	1·2
Chemicals	2·6
Engineering	**0·8**
Textiles and clothing	–1·6
GDP	2·2

Note: Real figures for sectors of manufacturing are generated by deflating nominal outputs by the deflator for manufacturing as a whole.

Source: Central Statistical Office.

A similar discrepancy in the performance of these three broad industry groups emerges when we examine their shares of OECD export markets in Figure 1. The chemical industries have held their share since 1970. Engineering's share of OECD markets has been declining, though it recovered a little in the later 1980s, and the

Figure 1: The Value of UK Exports as a Percentage of Total OECD Exports, 1970-89

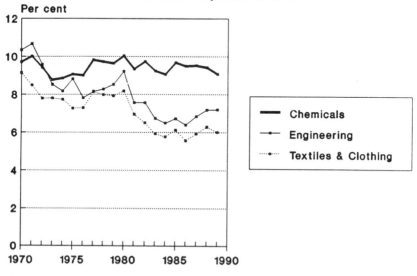

Source: OECD, CSO.

TABLE 2

GROWTH RATES OF THE ENGINEERING SECTORS, 1979-89

	Real average per cent change 1979-89
Other transport equipment mainly aerospace	3·9
Electrical and instrument engineering	2·4
Motor vehicles and parts	0·1
Metal goods	−0·6
Mechanical engineering	−1·0
GDP	2·2

Note: Real figures for sectors of engineering are generated by deflating nominal outputs by the deflator for manufacturing as a whole.

share of garments and textiles declined still more sharply than engineering.

The performance of engineering is clearly important, both because it constitutes a high fraction of manufacturing, and because it is probably the swing sector on which long-term recovery will turn. We are likely to continue to hold our own in chemicals and pharmaceuticals and to continue to have areas of considerable weakness. Our overall success is likely to turn on how far we can improve the economy's middling performers, and here engineering is crucial.

The engineering industry is made up of five broad sectors which have performed very differently. Table 2 shows that aerospace and electrical and instrument engineering have both grown faster than GDP, while the other three sectors, mechanical engineering, motor vehicles and parts, and metal goods have scarcely grown at all or have declined.

The UK has in fact performed extremely strongly in aerospace, where there was a substantial balance-of-payments surplus even in 1990 when trade in general was in massive deficit, and there has been considerable strength in electrical engineering. Mechanical engineering and metal goods have in contrast been weak, while motor vehicles, which appeared to be among the weakest in the mid-1980s, have staged a startling recovery under the especial stimulus of inward Japanese, French and United States investment. The enhanced quality standards imposed by these newcomers to the UK car industry have gone on to

TABLE 3

ENGINEERING SALES BY SECTOR:
ENGINEERING EMPLOYERS' FEDERATION
ESTIMATES FOR 1991

Sector	Sales £ billion	% of industry total
Electrical and Instrument Engineering	41·24	33·6
Mechanical Engineering	31·87	26·0
Motor Vehicles and Parts	21·73	17·7
Metal Goods	13·99	11·4
Other Transport Equipment including Aerospace	13·85	11·3
Total Engineering	122·68	100·0

TABLE 4

REAL GROWTH IN ENGINEERING OUTPUT, 1979-89

	Annual average per cent growth, 1979-89*
Japan	9·3
USA	4·1
Italy	2·9
Western Germany	1·6
UK	**0·8**
France	0·8

Note: *1979-87 for the USA, 1979-88 for Western Germany.
Source: *OECD National Accounts*, Vol. II; *CSO Blue Book*.

have a highly favourable impact on other car producers and upon the many companies in the immensely detailed supply chain involved in vehicle manufacturing. The size of the sectors that make up engineering is outlined in Table 3.

Because the sectors of the industry group have performed so differently, any general weaknesses that comparative international data show are entirely compatible with a superior British performance

TABLE 5

ENGINEERING OUTPUT AS A PERCENTAGE OF
GDP AT MARKET PRICES, 1970, 1979 AND 1989

	1970	1979	1989*
Western Germany	15·2	14·6	14·7
Japan	14·4	11·1	12·6
France	10·2	9·7	8·4
UK	**11·8**	**10·9**	**8·3**
Italy	8·4	10·3	8·3
USA	10·7	9·9	8·1

Note: *1988 for Western Germany, 1987 for USA.

Source: *OECD National Accounts*, Vol. II; UK figures are from the CSO.

in aerospace and considerable inferiority in some of the other areas.

Real growth in engineering output in the UK has been slower than our major competitors. Table 4 shows that amongst the six major industrialised countries, only France's engineering output has grown as slowly as the United Kingdom's.

The share of engineering output as a proportion of GDP has been falling over several decades. Table 5 shows that the UK's 3½ percentage points fall in the engineering industry's contribution to GDP at market prices since 1970 is by far the largest among the six major industrialised countries.

Whilst the engineering output growth rate of 0·8 per cent per annum between 1979 and 1989 is below the economy average, productivity has grown by more than 5 per cent a year; Table 6 shows that productivity has risen faster than in the engineering industries of Italy, France and West Germany. Because output growth has been modest whilst productivity growth has been exceptional, employment has declined especially rapidly in the engineering sector.

In 1970, 3·9 million people were employed in these industries. The workforce fell to 3·3 million in 1979 and to 2·3 million in 1989, which is about 9 per cent of total employment in the UK. Table 7 shows how the 30 per cent decline in employment over the last business cycle has been the most substantial among the six major industrialised countries.

TABLE 6

PRODUCTIVITY GROWTH IN ENGINEERING, 1979-89

	Average annual growth of real output per person (Per cent)*
Japan	7·0
USA	5·5
UK	**5·1**
Italy	4·7
France	3·0
Western Germany	1·2

Note: *1979-87 for USA, 1979-88 for Western Germany.

Source: *Blue Book* and *Census of Production*, Central Statistical Office (UK); *OECD National Accounts*.

TABLE 7

EMPLOYMENT IN THE ENGINEERING SECTOR, 1979 AND 1989
(*Thousands of employees*)

	1979	1989*	Per cent change
UK	**3,332**	**2,319**	**-30·4**
Italy	1,962	1,574	-19·8
France	2,198	1,773	-19·4
USA	8,986	8,300	-7·6
Western Germany	4,044	4,182	3·4
Japan	5,111	6,500	27·2

Note: *1988 for Western Germany.

Source: *OECD National Accounts*, Vol. II, 1989; CSO.

Investment and the Performance of the Engineering Industry

The amount of capital available to engineering workers has an important impact on their productivity. One indicator of this is investment behaviour in different countries which will be affected by the cost of capital and the profitability of companies.

Nominal interest rates have been higher in the UK than in

TABLE 8

REAL LONG-TERM INTEREST RATES, 1979-90

	1979	1982	1985	1988	1989	1990
USA	0·7	6·6	7·8	5·8	4·4	4·4
Japan	4·7	6·2	4·8	4·0	3·2	5·4
Western Germany	3·5	4·6	4·6	4·7	4·6	6·7
France	−0·8	4·0	5·1	6·1	5·4	7·6
UK	**−1·5**	**5·2**	**5·0**	**2·6**	2·7	**5·0**
Italy	−1·2	5·1	4·1	4·5	4·0	5·5

Note: Long-term government bond rate less inflation rate (GDP/GNP deflators used).

Source: *International Financial Statistics*, International Monetary Fund, and *OECD National Accounts*.

TABLE 9

GROSS OPERATING SURPLUS IN ENGINEERING
AS PERCENT OF VALUE-ADDED, 1979 AND 1989

	1979	1989*
Japan	38·3	42·5
Italy	33·9	37·8
France	24·3	26·3
Western Germany	25·2	26·3
UK	**13·7**	**25·4**
USA	20·5	19·9

Note: *1987 for the USA, 1986 for France, 1988 for Western Germany.

Source: *OECD National Accounts*, Vol. II, and *CSO Blue Book*.

competitor countries but, adjusted for inflation, real interest rates are not higher in the UK than elsewhere (see Table 8).

The data in Table 9 indicate that engineering is about as profitable on average in the UK (judged by the surplus of value-added over the compensation of employees) as in France and Germany, but there are sectors of UK engineering that are far less profitable than the average. Table 10 shows that electrical and instrument engineering is more than twice as profitable as any other sector, and that the profitability of the

TABLE 10

OPERATING SURPLUS NET OF CAPITAL CONSUMPTION
AS A PER CENT OF VALUE ADDED IN UK INDUSTRY,
1979 AND 1989

	1979	1989	Average 1985-89
Chemicals	27·7	40·4	40·3
Total Engineering	**8·6**	**21·0**	**17·1**
of which			
Electrical and instrument engineering	*17·8*	*25·3*	*26·7*
Mechanical engineering	*12·2*	*17·4*	*12·3*
Motor vehicles and parts	*–2·3*	*20·0*	*11·0*
Metal goods	*9·1*	*13·7*	*10·9*
Other transport equipment (including aerospace)	*–22·8*	*20·3*	*6·3*
Textiles and clothing	9·1	10·5	11·5
Total manufacturing	12·5	23·9	21·6

Note: Net operating surplus = gross value added – income from employment – capital consumption.

Net value added = gross value added – capital consumption.

Source: CSO.

other categories is extremely weak. Mechanical engineering and the general manufacture of cars, aircraft, etc., are far less profitable than manufacturing in general, let alone the growth areas such as chemicals with more than three times the profitability of mechanical engineering.

Investment in engineering in comparison with chemicals reflects the profitability gap set out in Table 10 (see Figure 2). The danger is that in the low profitability areas of engineering, which means most of the industry so far as employment is concerned, profitability is inadequate to sustain the high investment, R&D and new product development on which the future of the industry in Europe and the world so crucially depends.

There is no readily available international comparison of investment in engineering. Nevertheless, a comparative study of the engineering industry in the UK with the fabricated metal products, machinery and equipment sectors in Western Germany, France and the USA (comparable figures for Italy and Japan are not available) shows that the investment to output ratio in the UK, at between 9 and 12 per cent,

Figure 2: The Ratio of Gross Investment to Output in Engineering, Textiles and Chemicals, 1979-89

Source: CSO Blue Book.

Figure 3: Engineering Sector Investment to Output Ratio, 1979-89

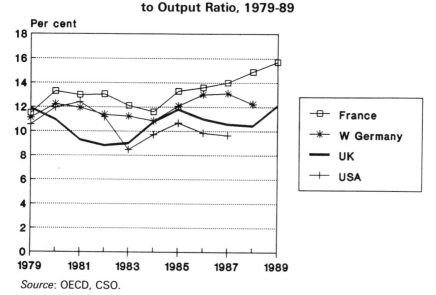

Source: OECD, CSO.

33

has been between 1 and 2 percentage points lower than in France and Germany, but it appears to be higher than investment in the US engineering industry (see Figure 3).

The Particular Problems of Aerospace and Capital Plant and the Transformation of Motor Vehicles

The UK aerospace industry has been the best performing of the engineering sectors. In 1989, turnover of the industry was £10·7 billion, it employed about 194,000 people, and the balance-of-payments surplus, whilst erratic, was £1·7 billion in 1990 (and £712 million in the first half of 1991).

Aerospace is the only engineering sector to have improved its balance-of-trade performance over the past decade, and the fall in employment has been considerably less than in other parts of engineering. Indeed, employment in the 'Other Transport Equipment' sector, about four-fifths of which was aerospace in the late 1980s, has been more resistant to economic downturns than other engineering sectors. Employment was actually higher in June 1991 than in June 1989.

Aerospace industries tend to be national champions with governments closely involved as sponsors, customers, specifiers and financiers. This means that government policies often have an overriding bearing on the industry's fortunes.

Defence has played a significant part in the development of the aerospace industry and the government has procured most military aircraft domestically, often collaborating with other European countries. In civil aircraft, the UK participates in Airbus Industrie and other international collaborative ventures. Aircraft manufacture is a capital-intensive industry with huge upfront investments in new products. These investments are recovered, if ever, only after many years of sales. This is why the UK, France, Germany and Spain joined together to form the Airbus consortium.

The aerospace sector, which has been the most successful in engineering, is now entering a critical phase because of the impending decline in defence procurements in the 1990s, and therefore in the corresponding support by government of research and development. But markets for civil aviation are certain to continue to grow and so to offer opportunities for growing sales. Our aerospace companies have had to wean themselves increasingly from the world of closed Ministry of Defence contracts, protected by secrecy from some of the pressures of international competition. Their success in the 1990s will depend on the extent to which they can accelerate their cultural shift from defence and closed government contracts and on how far they can get the details of their European collaboration right.

The construction and manufacture of capital plant, which is responsible for about one-tenth of total engineering output, also merits attention. Here a good deal of the industry has been accustomed to supplying the large British public utilities which have automatically turned to British suppliers for power stations and similar large installations. Most of these public utilities have now been privatised, and all are now required by the European Public Purchasing Directives to throw contracts open to European competition. This will open up national markets that have long been rigged in favour of domestic industries. The UK has been a pioneer in opening these markets, and our own plant imports, especially in the electricity supply industry, have begun to grow. To succeed in the more competitive markets we are moving towards, a cultural change will be required in this important area of the engineering industry.

Turnaround in the UK Automotive Industry

The sector of engineering that has actually achieved a true cultural advance is the automotive industry. Ten years ago observers of the UK car industry had largely written it off. From 1972 to 1982, UK production of passenger cars fell by 54 per cent and a small trade surplus turned into a deficit of £2 billion. The British-owned volume producers had been merged into British Leyland, which was rapidly losing market share at home and abroad. Multinational companies such as Ford and General Motors (Vauxhall) were increasingly supplying the UK market from their Continental rather than local plants. The UK's car industry was known for poor labour relations, scandalous labour practices and unacceptable quality.

Yet in the next three or four years the foundations were laid for a remarkable turnaround which started to be reflected in the figures from about 1989 onwards. The volume of imports dropped by 10 per cent in 1990 and by a further 31 per cent in 1991 (January to November comparison). This was, of course, in a market which declined by 13 per cent and 21 per cent in these years. However, the volume of exports in 1990 and 1991 increased by 20 per cent and 28 per cent in a world market that in itself was at best stable. The increase in the actual numbers of vehicles produced for export in 1991 is even more startling—60 per cent.

The difference between number and volume is accounted for by a tripling of exports in the smaller car category, offset to some extent by a 34 per cent reduction of exports of larger cars. It is, of course, amongst the smaller cars that Japan has had the greatest positive effect on the UK's performance and in luxury cars where much of the European industry, perhaps mistakenly, sees its salvation.

This improvement in trade performance has meant the production of over 400,000 extra vehicles, 30 per cent of total production in the UK in 1991. As a result, production levels have fallen by only 3 per cent from 1990 despite a severely depressed home market. In passing, it must be noted that maintaining production levels does not save the industry from pain, since the 400,000 extra vehicles represent some shift from established producers to new ones and from Continental to British plants. In a highly competitive industry in which world-wide capacity is growing, and demand in 1991 was suppressed, employment can be maintained only with growing production volumes, and profit is vulnerable. 1991 has been a painful year for the industry in the UK, but it would have been much more uncomfortable without the change in performance.

This has two main causes. In the 1980s there was a major improvement in labour relations and management capability in Britain. Yet that improvement was equally available to the rest of the engineering industry which did not avail itself of this opportunity to the same extent as the car industry. The second cause was the coming of the Japanese. They have stimulated the performance of the UK's industry in four ways: direct investment; joint ventures; competitive examples; and development of the supply infrastructure. These will be considered in turn.

Impact of UK Production of Japanese Cars

The three leading Japanese producers, Toyota, Nissan and Honda, are all investing in vehicle production in the UK. By 1995 their combined capacity will be between 400,000 and 500,000 vehicles and plans for the year 2000 approach 1 million units. Some part of this will substitute for existing production by their competitors in Britain, but the major part will replace imports from Japan or represent new exports, mainly to Continental Europe. In 1990 and 1991, however, only Nissan was actually producing here and its contribution was 76,000 and 120,000 vehicles in these two years. Over 90 per cent of Nissan's 1991 output was exported, but its presence in the UK market was affected by a

Figure 4: Comparison of Passenger Car and Total Manufacturing Export/Import Ratios, 1985-91

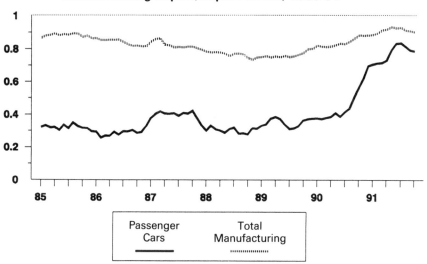

Note: Three-month moving average.

Source: CSO.

change of distribution arrangements—over the longer term Nissan UK expects to export about 70 per cent of production. If the Japanese-owned plants do produce 1 million vehicles and export 70 per cent, this country has the potential of being a net exporter of cars within 10 years. The trade balance has in any case been transformed, as Figure 4 shows.

In addition to Nissan's 120,000 vehicles, the rest of the industry also performed well in 1991. In part, this was the result of a joint venture: Honda has a 20 per cent shareholding in Rover, the two companies work closely together, and Rover has transformed its manufacturing practices as a result of this experience. Rover also produces Honda-designed vehicles and adapts Honda designs. This illustrates another specific strength of the Japanese, which is their ability to design vehicles that can be produced economically and consistently to a high level of quality. Although the UK has proved a fertile location for Japanese production techniques and procedures, design practices have not yet been successfully transferred.

The greatest stimulus provided by the Japanese in the period under consideration has been through the effect of competition. Companies such as Ford and General Motors, which have lost market share in the

United States and elsewhere, have responded very vigorously and made considerable efforts to learn from the Japanese through joint ventures and simple imitation. In their UK plants, the effect has been one of considerable improvement in quality and productivity, which has enabled the companies concerned to maintain or increase the proportion of their European production carried out in their British plants. However, these lessons have been available to all the national subsidiaries of the multinational companies. It is interesting and important to know why the UK appears to have benefited disproportionately. Why, for example, should the Ryton plant of Peugeot—which under the ownership of Rootes and Chrysler was an indifferent performer—have become one of the best plants in the Peugeot group, increasing production from 46,000 vehicles in 1987 to 117,000 in 1990?

Low Labour Costs in Britain Compared with Germany

Clearly, an important factor is the combination of relatively low labour costs and the improved industrial relations climate previously referred to. The German Motor Industry Association estimated that labour costs per hour in the UK in 1990 were the lowest in Europe and nearly 40 per cent below those of Western Germany, the principal car producer in Europe. This is an important factor, both in new inward investment and in the choice of production location for established multinationals.

An exceptional item is the 36 per cent growth in the German market in 1991 as a result of unification. After 1991 the market is forecast to return to more normal levels, but during the year German capacity has been fully engaged and a rare opportunity given to other producers. It is encouraging and may be significant that the British producers have been more successful than most in taking this opportunity. French production fell by 6 per cent in a home market that declined by 10 per cent, whilst Italian production fell by 12 per cent in a home market that remained virtually stable. UK production fell by 3 per cent in a market that declined by 20 per cent.

Thus, the British motor industry has improved its performance relative to its rivals. One reason could be the openness of our economy and the extent to which competition has been felt by the industry. The Fiat Group, for example, had 67 per cent of its sales in 1990 in the protected Italian market and fully 78 per cent in the more protected markets of Europe (France, Italy and Spain). Renault had 49 per cent of its sales in the home market and 73 per cent in protected markets. In contrast, the UK market has long been open, with imports accounting for more than 50 per cent. The high level of inward investment from Japan has exposed competitors and managers in this country to Japanese management practices to a much greater degree than in any other European country.

Suppliers in the UK have also been exposed to Japanese practices. The Japanese automotive industry has obtained a competitive edge through working very closely with its suppliers. All manufacturers are looking for cheaper and better components, but whereas the Western companies have sought these through competition between suppliers, Japanese companies have generally put pressure on, and given management and technical support to single suppliers. In 1991 Nissan Manufacturing (UK) spent £450 million on bought-in supplies, £350 million of it in the UK, 40 per cent of which was local to the plant in the North of England. Nissan works closely with its suppliers to improve technical and managerial capability and reports that the leading ones are reaching international standards. Rover and General Motors have moved towards the Japanese purchasing model and Ford and Peugeot are also active in supplier development.

Japanese investment in European component supply is much less than in vehicle manufacture. The opportunities for both business and for performance improvement through partnership sourcing are available to established companies in this country and are being seized by them. Component companies, which improve through serving Nissan, are available to serve the other manufacturers. In this way they contribute to the escalating standards of performance in the UK's automotive industry.

The Quality of the Workforce and the Performance of Engineering

The quality of its managers, engineers and craftsmen is a vital factor in the performance of the engineering industry. This is being transformed in the automotive sector but much of the industry complains of a difficulty in attracting a high quality workforce. This is not surprising when the evidence of what most of the industry pays is examined. There is evidence that careers in engineering and science are not the most attractive option for many graduates. Table 11, which draws on the most recent data, indicates that the industries to which most engineering and science graduates are recruited have a lower typical salary progression than areas such as banking and financial services.

TABLE 11

AVERAGE TOTAL EARNINGS FOR AN 'ACCEPTABLE' AND
'ABOVE AVERAGE' PERFORMER BY INDUSTRY

(*£s*)

Industry Sector	'Acceptable' Performer		'Above Average' Performer	
	after 6 months	after 5 years	after 6 months	after 5 years
Computer and Electronics	13,443	21,318	14,099	25,154
Financial Services	12,313	21,214	12,358	23,195
Banks	12,060	19,021	12,579	23,284
Insurance	11,798	17,433	11,997	19,247
Chemical and Allied Industries	12,305	17,138	11,419	19,442
Engineering (incl. Auto)	11,604	17,004	12,031	19,410
Construction	13,070	16,778	13,195	17,963

Source: PA Survey of Graduate Salaries, 1990/91.

TABLE 12

AVERAGE TOTAL EARNINGS FOR AN 'ACCEPTABLE' AND
AN 'ABOVE AVERAGE' PERFORMER BY FUNCTION

(*£s*)

Function	'Acceptable' Performer		'Above Average' Performer	
	after 6 months	after 5 years	after 6 months	after 5 years
Electronic Engineering	14,647	23,154	14,925	26,524
Accountancy	10,917	22,302	10,917	25,876
Computing	12,815	20,487	13,795	23,778
Sales and Marketing	12,432	19,311	12,934	23,545
Research and Development	12,105	16,817	12,449	20,119
Mechanical Engineering	11,970	16,524	12,200	17,596

Source: PA Survey of Graduate Salaries, 1990/91.

TABLE 13

GRADUATE EARNINGS IN SELECTED OCCUPATIONS AS A
RATIO OF AVERAGE NON-MANUAL EARNINGS, 1976-88

Years	Chartered Engineers	Chemists	Physicists	Business Economists	Lawyers in Industry	Accountants in Industry
1976	1·48	1·64	1·67	2·07[1]	2·01	1·03
1978	1·43	1·57	1·54[2]		2·01	1·11
1980	1·43	1·52	1·54	1·97[2]	2·12	1·12
1982	1·43	1·51	1·54		2·24	1·13[3]
1984	1·41	1·56	1·56[4]	1·92	2·30	1·18
1986	1·39	1·50	1·53[5]	2·10	2·37	1·24
1988	1·38	1·42	1·36	2·08	2·51[5]	1·28

Note: [1] 1974.   [2] 1979.   [3] 1981.   [4] 1985.   [5] 1987.

Source: D. Bosworth and R. Wilson (1990), University of Warwick (mimeo).

Engineers with computing skills and potential can, however, achieve very high incomes and the Table shows a sharp divide between mechanical engineering and electronic engineering. The picture is confirmed by an examination of pay variations between what people do in their companies. Table 12 indicates that graduates employed in research and development and as engineers tend to experience less salary growth than those involved in accountancy, computing, sales and marketing. For example, a typical engineer will earn around 9 per cent more than an accountant after six months service but 35 per cent less after five years. Finally, there is also evidence that the relative earnings of scientists and engineers have been slipping in the last decade. Table 13 provides evidence that the pay of these groups has declined relative to average non-manual earnings and other groups employed in industry such as business economists, accountants and lawyers.

Pay differentials are one indicator of the extent to which employers give young people early responsibility. Most able young people are attracted by the thought of being challenged and their perceptions of different employers in this regard influence their choice of profession and company. The relatively low educational qualifications of British managers in several industries including engineering, when compared with those of our major trading competitors, has been well documented.

TABLE 14

INTERNATIONAL COMPARISON OF SKILL SHORTAGES:
PERCENTAGE OF FIRMS CONSTRAINED
BY SKILL SHORTAGES, 1987-89

	UK	W. Germany	France	Italy	Netherlands
1987	**21·00**	2·75	2·75	1·00	2·50
1988	**26·25**	3·00	3·75	2·00	1·50
1989	**19·25**	6·75	5·25	2·75	2·75

Source: European Commission.

It may be that the less well educated manager lacks the confidence or ability to attract and utilise properly educated first-rate people. If this is so, it will be reflected in over-rigid pay scales and an unwillingness to pay the market-clearing rates necessary to ameliorate problems of skill shortage.

The long-term persistence of some shortages of skilled labour and graduates with particular areas of expertise suggests that the appropriate pay signals are not always generated. To illustrate this, consider the proportion of firms constrained by skill shortages in different manufacturing industries, as reported in the 1979-90 CBI Industrial Trends Surveys. If firms pushed up relative earnings to reduce skill shortages in the fashion predicted by supply and demand analysis, one would expect average earnings in the industries with the highest average skill shortages to rise relative to other industries. There has been a positive response to the shortage of those with computing skills and to skill shortages in the electronic engineering sector, but no evident response to the perceived skill shortages in mechanical engineering. Pay has evidently been flexible enough to solve only some of the skill shortage problems.

Skill Shortages Are More Severe in the UK

Persistent reported skill shortages seem to be more serious in the UK than in some of its competitors, as Table 14 indicates. This evidence is consistent with the UK having a relatively unskilled labour force, making employers search longer for people of a given skill level, and pay not being used to close the gap between supply and demand. Table 15 shows that the occupations with the greatest 'shortages' problems are those of engineers and technologists; some of the occupations on

TABLE 15

THE 10 TOP OCCUPATIONS WITH 'HARD TO FILL' VACANCIES (ESTABLISHMENTS WITH 25 PLUS EMPLOYEES)

	% of total 'hard to fill' vacancies
Engineers and technologists	10
Scientific technicians	3
Health associate professional (mainly nurses)	5
Metal machining, fitting, instrument-making trades	3
Electrical/electronic trades	3
Textiles, garment and related trades	6
Catering occupations	3
Secretaries, personal assistants, typists, WP operators	7
General occupations in service/sales (e.g. porters)	5
Sales assistants/checkout operators	4
TOTAL	49

Source: IFF Research Limited.

the list suffer a problem because of a lack of qualified people, others because of relatively low pay. The case of engineers and technologists is sufficiently important to merit further investigation, as a case study in the relationship between industry and education, and we now turn to this subject.

Engineering manpower is recognised as being of critical importance to developed industrial economies. Whilst international comparisons of engineering skills are difficult to undertake, there are some indications that the UK suffers from a relative disadvantage in the flow of such skills to the economy. Table 16 indicates that six years ago the UK was producing fewer engineering qualifications at all levels, but particularly in craft-level skills.

The long-run pay and career prospects of engineering graduates have been relatively poor, and this has plausibly led to the reduced interest by young people in engineering careers. It is notable that the volume of applications and applicants for engineering and technology degrees has not kept pace with the much increased demand for higher education, and the average 'A'-level scores of university entrants in mathematics and engineering have been falling since the mid-1980s.

TABLE 16

NUMBERS QUALIFYING IN ENGINEERING
AND TECHNOLOGY, 1985

(*Thousands*)

	UK	France	W. Germany
First Degrees	14	15	21
Technician	30	35	44
Craft	36	91	120

Source: *Employment in Europe*, European Commission, 1990.

In addition to paying engineering graduates well, engineering skill levels in Germany are substantially augmented by the presence of technically qualified *Meisters* of a craft background but with the necessary skills to resolve routine maintenance and technical problems as they occur. This results in improved productivity and quality but also avoids calling in qualified engineers to deal with such problems. In the UK they are frequently brought in to deal with relatively routine problems, and this represents a further example of the poor utilisation of skills which leads to an inability on the part of employers to pay adequately or to make the jobs sufficiently interesting.

Craft-Level Skills Gap Between UK and Germany

The greatest perceived engineering skills gap between Germany, France and the UK lies at the craft level, in occupations at (broadly) National Vocational Qualifications Level 3. It is estimated that Germany and France respectively produce three and two-and-a-half times as many craft-level qualifications as the UK. As a result, the ratio of higher-than-craft to craft engineering qualifications in France and Germany is 1:2 whilst the UK ratio is 2:1. The contraction in engineering craft apprenticeships in the 1980s has contributed to this situation, and it has been argued that trainee income and rates of return to engineering trainees in the UK are significantly higher than in Germany, depressing the supply of engineering apprenticeships. This perceived market failure may also result from inflexible wage structures, and poor career opportunities affecting the demand for traineeships.

A number of meticulous studies of matched engineering and other manufacturing plants over the last decade has established that there is a

TABLE 17

NUMBERS OBTAINING ENGINEERING AND TECHNOLOGY
QUALIFICATIONS AT INTERMEDIATE LEVEL IN
UK, FRANCE AND GERMANY, 1986

(*Thousands*)

	UK	France	Germany
Higher technician/Meister	23	22	44
Lower technician	14	19	–
Craftworkers	27	107	107
Total	64	148	151

French total standardised for size of workforce.

Source: National Institute Economic Review (1991), p. 61.

strong relationship between high productivity and the skills of the
workforce. It is notable that the UK compares poorly with Germany
and France in the numbers of people obtaining engineering and
technology qualifications, at intermediate level (Table 17).

Another indicator of the relative skills position of UK engineering is
the existing stock of qualified employees at various levels. Figures for
all manufacturing suggest that a lower proportion of intermediate-level
employees has qualifications relative to the situation in France and
Germany. For example, in 1988, 31 per cent of British technicians had
no vocational qualification, compared to just 8 per cent of German
technicians (in 1987).

The poor skills position of the engineering industry may be caused
by the decline in the number of apprentices in the last decade (Figure
5), though there has been a slight rise in recent years. This decline has
been balanced by the increase in Youth Training Scheme numbers and
by the increased propensity of young people to remain in part-time or
full-time education. Both these developments will result in an increase
in the skills which can be attracted to the engineering industry.

Fall in Company Training in Engineering

The number of those gaining engineering and technology qualifications is only one indicator of the skills position in the industry,
particularly as many firms are more interested in training employees to
company standards rather than certifying those skills externally.
However, there is little evidence from the industry that the proportion

Figure 5: Young People Registered for Craft and Technician Training in the Engineering Industry, 1979-89

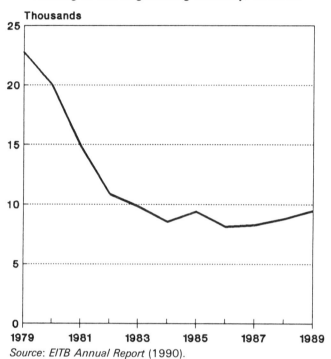

Source: *EITB Annual Report* (1990).

of employees receiving training in recent years has significantly increased.

Indeed, according to the annual survey conducted by the Engineering Industry Training Board, the total number of persons receiving training during the 1980s was halved—from 159,054 in 1980 to 64,196 in 1990. This fall was more severe than the contraction in total engineering employment. Figure 6 demonstrates the decline in the proportion of people receiving training on a spot day in April from 1979 to 1990. It also shows that the decline in the number of people receiving training is even more severe in the craft and technician categories where training is traditionally more concentrated. However, it is also believed that increased informal training and the development of open learning, for instance, are not reflected in the figures. It is therefore difficult to be precise about trends in training in the industry.

The competence of first-line managers in helping to identify the

Figure 6: Percentage of Engineering Employees Receiving Training, 1979-90

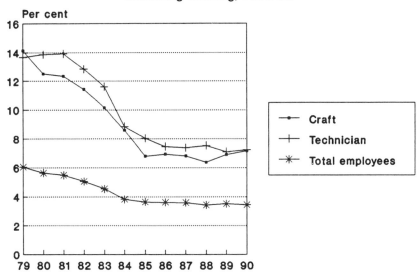

Source: Engineering Industry Training Board.

skills needs of the workforce and match them to the competitive requirements of the business, has been widely recognised. However, the evidence is that UK engineering supervisors are poorly prepared for this rôle. A high proportion does not obtain recognised qualifications of any kind and the existing supervisory qualifications do not provide the technical competence that so many supervisors lack (Table 18).

The Challenge to the Engineering Industry

Much of the UK engineering industry has been performing less well than manufacturing industry as a whole. But there have been high performing sectors and the most hopeful development has been the significant turnaround in the car industry. The National Economic Development Council's Engineering Industry Sector Group, chaired by Bill Jordan, President of the Amalgamated Engineering Union, and the Engineering Skills Working Party, chaired by Ian Gibson, Chief Executive of Nissan UK, recently presented a joint paper to the NEDC which covered much of this ground and recommended a programme of action for the whole industry. That programme was accepted by the Government, the CBI and the TUC. The challenge for the industry

TABLE 18

PERCENTAGE OF MANUFACTURING FOREMEN
WITH QUALIFICATIONS:
UK, FRANCE (1988) AND GERMANY (1987)

	UK	France	Germany
No vocational qualifications	55	44	7
Intermediate vocational qualification	42	55	93
Degree or equivalent	3	1	–

Source: National Institute Economic Review (1991), p. 64.

which is addressed in the programme is to apply throughout engineering the management practices which are turning round the automotive industry.

Many companies are reluctant to adopt what are seen as management practices rooted in an alien culture. Some have adopted very specific techniques and become disillusioned because they do not yield their full benefit in the absence of an appropriate management environment. Yet the potential benefits are considerable. Labour productivity in the majority of European vehicle producers is half of that achieved by Japanese producers in the UK. Repairs under warranty in the first year are twice as high in much of Europe as in Nissan here. The essence of the Japanese approach is to give everyone in the organisation the skills, motivation and tools to solve problems as they arise and to search for better methods of performing their tasks. It is a relentless search for continuous improvement.

NEDC's Initiative to Promote 'Best Practice'

The two NEDC Committees, which have high credibility in the industry because they include the Chairmen and Chief Executives of several major companies in their membership, will research and codify best practice in the UK and promote it to the industry. They will work with government, trade unions and industry bodies. In particular, they will work with companies at the head of the supply chain to improve the performance of their suppliers. The information will be made available to companies in a form in which they can use it, but ultimately it is companies themselves which must decide how they apply this knowledge. The application is not simple or procedural—it involves a profound cultural change for the majority of businesses.

The Engineering Skills Working Party will work with the established institutions to identify the changes in skills needed to support this process, and to ensure that they can be delivered to the industry. Again, the effectiveness of this programme will depend upon the response of companies and their willingness to develop and use people appropriately. An important part of this is the way that companies reward and employ their professional staff, for if they do not recognise the contribution that good engineers make to the engineering industry, they cannot complain when too few good people wish to enter engineering. If they will not pay first-rate salaries, they cannot expect to get as many high-quality engineers and skilled craftsmen as the Japanese, German and US industries.

The changes required are difficult but achievable and the prize to be won is a transformation in the performance of much of the engineering industry, which is so central to the UK's future prosperity.

Devaluation Does Not Offer a Soft Macro Option

Other contributors to the discussion of the principal issues that face the UK see the lowering of interest rates by 2 percentage points and a devaluation of sterling to DM2·70 or below as the starting point of a solution. It is argued in this paper that the principal challenge to much of the engineering industry is to translate Japanese and other international best practice, which has been so effective in parts of the automotive industry, to the remainder of engineering and indeed to go on to achieve a similar transformation in other industries. Devaluation would contribute nothing to this target, and the automotive industry's growing export share at current exchange rates shows how the benefits from restructuring can be achieved with sterling at DM2·95, which must therefore be a level at which the right managerial decisions can be taken to make apparently weak British industries competitive.

Few economic relationships are better documented than the one that shows that devaluations raise inflation. They always have, because they allow businesses to be soft on pay and price increases, and there is no doubt that if sterling was reduced to DM2·70, Britain's rate of inflation would rise. It is also certain that if Britain entered a higher inflation league, UK interest rates would have to rise. Those who wish to devalue might succeed in lowering interest rates for a few weeks, but even that is doubtful. As soon as the rate of inflation the foreign exchange market expected rose—and this should happen immediately—interest rates would be likely to rise to a level considerably above

Germany's. Countries in the third division inflation league have interest rates approximately 5 percentage points above those of countries like Germany which have near price stability, which is where Britain's interest rates were in the years of double-digit inflation. Countries with 2 or 3 percentage points more inflation than Germany—and that has generally been the British situation—have to have interest rates 2 or 3 percentage points above Germany's. The devaluers are bound to raise UK inflation, and if it again rose significantly above Germany's, this would be certain to lead to higher British interest rates in the 1990s.

Every country in the world has an economic cycle. In the boom phase there is a considerable risk that inflation will rise; in the recession phase inflation comes down. One characteristic of an influential group within the British economics profession is that the recession phase of the cycle is regarded as just the right time to devalue, so British recessions in the 1960s and 1970s were not used to get inflation down. Instead UK inflation rose in most recessions because sterling was continually devalued. This happened on several occasions and it is extraordinary that there are now those who propose a repetition of this error. They hope, of course, that the inflation that devaluation causes in recession will be corrected through remarkable growth in the subsequent boom, but this has never occurred. Inflation has always risen in British booms, as it has overseas.

Conclusion

The vital need for British industry and the economy in the 1990s is another nine-year period of expansion to repeat the uninterrupted growth from 1981 until 1990. With sustainable expansion which continues for nearly a decade, there will be an appropriate economic environment for industrial restructuring. If instead the economy is kick-started into some kind of boom with a considerable relaxation of fiscal policy and an accompanying devaluation, inflation will accelerate, the balance of payments will deteriorate (because any excess of public and private investment over public and private saving is bound to produce an equivalent current account deficit), and the next government will have to kill the boom in its second or third year. This has happened on several occasions in the past and a characteristic of these hectic two- or three-year booms has been that virtually no industrial restructuring was achieved. That the next British recovery should last nine years is therefore far more important than the particular month in which it begins. It is vital to create the foundations for sustainable expansion rather than to jerk the economy around with the British propensity for fine tuning, and for devaluation whenever falling inflation produces temporary economic distress.

Economic re-expansion, when it comes, should be used to transfer what is being learned from the Japanese in the automotive industry to the bulk of mechanical engineering and to other industries. These developments will take time and they will require an environment of economic stability and of steady and sustainable low inflationary expansion.

4

THE HOUSING MARKET

Mark Boléat

Director-General,
The Council of Mortgage Lenders

Introduction

THE HOUSING MARKET is currently very depressed and commentators predict that it will remain depressed for the next year or so. There have already been a number of casualties, not just the 80,000 or so people whose homes were repossessed last year, but also among the builders and the lending institutions. A number of builders have gone bankrupt. Some of the foreign banks have decided that the mortgage market is not the profitable market that it seemed a few years ago, and even some of the building societies have found the going too tough.

This paper briefly surveys the current state of the housing and mortgage markets and predicts how they might move over the next year or so. It then analyses the package of policy initiatives announced by the Government and the Council of Mortgage Lenders over the last few months.

The Current Market

The British housing market is currently bumping along the bottom of what is generally agreed to be the deepest recession in living memory. The number of transactions in 1990 was 35 per cent below the peak level in 1988, and the final figures for 1991 are likely to show a further 10 per cent decline. The number of transactions currently taking place in the market is less than was the case in 1981 even though the owner-occupied housing stock has increased by 29 per cent in the past decade. Private sector housing starts in 1991 were about 135,000, the same as in 1990 and nearly 40 per cent below the peak of 221,000 recorded in 1988. In many parts of the country house prices have fallen back by 20 per cent or more from the peak figures recorded in 1988 or 1989.

The situation is even worse in the mortgage market. In money terms, net advances fell 17 per cent between 1988 and 1990 and a further fall occurred last year. The fall in the number of advances is even greater.

Statistics for arrears and repossessions are the most visible manifestation of the current depressed state of the market. In 1980 mortgage lenders took possession of under 4,000 properties. In 1989 the figure was 15,800, and in 1990 it was 43,890. The best estimate for 1991 is about 80,000 and, before the recent package of measures, some commentators were predicting a further increase in 1992.

The reasons for the current recession are fairly obvious and need be mentioned only briefly here. The housing market rose to unsustainable heights in 1987 and 1988, with the froth at the top being caused by a combination of interest rates being driven down to unrealistically low levels, sharp reductions in the higher rates of tax in the 1988 Budget, the way in which double tax relief was withdrawn in the summer of 1988, and also lax lending by some lenders (although, of course, that does not explain why people were willing to borrow in the first place). There was, in short, an unrealistic expectation that housing would always be a good investment and that the fundamentals no longer mattered.

Factors in the Housing Market Depression

A downturn was inevitable but the extent of the downturn has been greater than any commentator thought possible. Several factors can be identified which have contributed to this situation:

o   The fact that inflation is at a lower level than it has been in earlier housing downturns has made the adjustment of real house prices more difficult. It is relatively easy to secure a 20 per cent reduction in real house prices when inflation is 20 per cent but very difficult if inflation is running at only 5 per cent.

o The sharp increase in mortgage interest rates from 9·5 to 15 per cent in an 18-month period from the Spring of 1988 to the Autumn of 1989 both caused financial difficulties for some home buyers and served as a salutary lesson for all potential home buyers that mortgage interest rates could rise sharply.

o The value of mortgage tax relief has been progressively eroded by the maintenance of the £30,000 ceiling and reductions in tax rates. The impact of mortgage rate increases has therefore not been cushioned as much as used to be the case, and the holding of mortgages is no ionger as attractive as it used to be.

o There is now in London, and to a lesser extent in other parts of the country, a viable private rental market which gives people an alternative to owner-occupation.

o The recession in the economy generally has been more severe than had been forecast, particularly in London and the South East.

Recessions involve a circular process by which symptoms become causes and causes are themselves symptoms. This is particularly true of the impact of repossessions on the housing market. People fall into arrears with their loans because they are unable to meet the mortgage payments. Generally, this results either from relationship breakdown or severe loss of income. Repossessions, which generally follow heavy arrears (although they need not), result largely from a separate factor, that is, the relationship between the value of the house and the size of the outstanding loan. When house prices have increased rapidly a borrower with substantial arrears can trade out of the problem by selling, paying off the arrears and buying a cheaper property or, if it is open to him, moving into rented accommodation. By contrast, when house prices have fallen borrowers in arrears do not have this option. Furthermore, some people may be pushed into arrears simply because they have been unable to sell their house. For example, people may move for job reasons, financing the purchase of a new home with a bridging loan. They may then be unable to sell their previous home, and the strain of meeting two mortgage repayments causes them to fall into arrears. In such circumstances a much higher proportion of arrears leads to repossession and one can even have the phenomenon, which is now evident in some cases, that is, of people making an economic decision to default on their mortgage because they can benefit financially by so doing.

Not only is the current high level of repossessions a consequence of what is happening in the housing market; to some extent it is also a cause. The large number of houses which have been taken into possession by lenders have to be sold. They represent, like new houses, a net addition to the supply of housing to the market. Thus, unlike most housing transactions, the sale of one house does not lead directly to the purchase of another. The normal movement within the housing market has been lost. More generally, many people are unwilling to begin the process of buying until they feel confident that they can sell their house, thus further depressing the market. The depressed market in turn means people are more likely to default because they are unable to sell their home.

The Market in 1992

There can be little doubt that the housing and mortgage markets will remain relatively depressed in 1992, although there is a reasonable expectation that there will be a modest pick-up of activity.

On the supply side, there is currently a huge stock of housing available for sale which will be more than sufficient to absorb any increase in demand. Builders have some 70,000 or so completed, but unsold, houses, and mortgage lenders probably have a similar number of properties which they have taken into possession and have not yet sold. In addition, estate agents have large stocks on their books, and in the event of there being an increase in demand, additional supply would quickly come forward as those who have deferred selling for whatever reason put their houses on the market.

Given this scenario it is, perhaps, surprising that builders are forecasting an increase in starts in 1992, and, indeed, there has been evidence of such an increase over the last few months. It needs to be remembered here that builders may start new houses not with the expectation of making a profit, but rather in the short term to improve their cash flow. It can make economic sense for a builder to build a house even though he knows when he lays the first brick that he will make a loss. The land costs, which frequently were paid some time previously, together with rolled-up interest, must be regarded as sunk costs, and the calculation to the builder when deciding whether to start is whether the costs of building the house will more than be recovered by the expected sale price.

Threat of Unemployment Weakens Demand

Demand, in the short term at least, is expected to remain relatively weak. While the economy is beginning to move out of recession, as far as the housing market is concerned unemployment is one of the key variables, and this will continue to rise for much of 1992. As long as people fear that they might lose their jobs, this will be a factor influencing any decision to purchase a house. There has also been a significant structural change which needs to be considered. In London and the South East, in general most people in the past did not consider the possibility of becoming unemployed, but now everyone must consider this possibility, and perhaps this could lead to a permanent downward shift in the demand curve.

In the short term, an additional factor constraining demand may well be the current debate on taxation should the Labour Party win the General Election. It is not necessary to take sides as to what tax rates should be, still less as to what they might be, but it must be true that if people earning £20,000 plus per annum are contemplating house purchase, then they will be influenced by press comment to the effect that their tax bills might increase substantially. The reduction in tax rates in the 1988 Budget had a material effect on the demand for housing, so the prospect of higher taxes, whether that prospect is real or not, may well be having a depressing effect on demand.

Another structural factor which serves to weaken demand is doubt as to whether housing will be the good investment in the future that it has been in the past. The unique tax position of housing has been progressively eroded over a number of years, in particular through holding the tax relief ceiling constant and through more generous application of capital gains tax exemptions to other investments. The experience of the last few years has also been a factor.

Finally, even where people have wished to move up market they have been deterred from so doing because of doubts as to whether they could sell their existing home. This factor has led, to some extent, to an artificial market in which people are deterred from buying because they cannot sell, and the reason they cannot sell is because people are deterred from buying because they fear that they cannot sell.

Lower Prices, Wider Choice

While there are these factors depressing demand, there are others which should be stimulating it. House prices have come down very considerably, and can no longer be considered expensive in relation to earnings. Moreover, there are so many properties on the market that potential house buyers not only have a wide choice, but are also able to drive extremely good bargains in some cases. As well as house prices having come down, mortgage rates are also relatively low, at least compared with the very high rates recorded a few years ago. Mortgage lenders and house builders are offering a variety of special deals to stimulate demand further.

Putting the supply and demand factors together suggests that there will be a recovery of the market during 1992, but it is likely to be a relatively modest one. It may well be that when the uncertainty of the General Election is out of the way, some people who have been holding back on purchasing housing, either for the first time or in moving up the market, will be encouraged to do so. If there are further falls in interest rates, which is something that is not unreasonable given the current differential between UK and foreign interest rates, and the forecasts for inflation, then this will further stimulate demand.

Policy Initiatives

The last six months have seen a flurry of activity in respect of public policy towards the mortgage market. The Government has, rightly, been concerned at the developing problem. It must be a matter for public policy when significant numbers of people are losing their homes through inability to repay their mortgages, and, of course, there is also the cost to central government through income support, and to central and local government through the need to rehouse people who have lost their homes as a result of mortgage default. The present situation can also be seen as something of a political embarrassment to the Government which has been so committed to home ownership. Mortgage lenders have been equally concerned to do something about the problem. As organisations which have been in business to help people become owner-occupiers, they simply do not like taking possession and regard this as a failure. In addition, of course, the high level of arrears is very costly to them.

Government and mortgage lenders, through the Council of Mortgage Lenders, have been working together with the objective of reducing the number of possessions, and thereby reducing the impact which repossessed properties have on the housing market. The first initiative to be announced, in November 1991, was a scheme for housing associations to take over the management of properties in possession. While not directly reducing the number of people who might lose their homes, this scheme would provide an additional source of supply for local authorities and housing associations to help house homeless families, and it would also serve to take some houses out of the owner-occupation market.

Direct Payment of Income Support for Mortgages?

For mortgage lenders, the main objective in these discussions has been to obtain direct payment of income support. The current social security system provides for mortgage borrowers otherwise eligible for income support—broadly speaking, those not in full-time employment—to obtain an additional benefit to meet interest incurred on loans for house purchase, with half of the interest being met in the first 16 weeks of a claim, and the full amount thereafter. The cost of income support has, of course, risen dramatically over the last few years, reaching an estimated £750 million in 1991. Income support is paid to the borrower, and the lender may well not know that the borrower is receiving it. Lenders estimate that no more than half of income support payments paid specifically in respect of mortgage interest reach them. If this is correct, then a significant proportion of repossessions, certainly over one-fifth, are caused directly by people obtaining a state benefit to meet their mortgage interest payments, and not using it for that purpose.

Mortgage lenders have been pressing government to introduce direct payment for some 15 years, but it has been the strong view at the Department of Social Security that this would go against the wish for people to be responsible for their own finances. However, following lengthy discussions, the DSS did agree in November last year to major changes in the administrative arrangements for paying income support. The new arrangements, which are now in effect, ensure that mortgage lenders are on notice that borrowers are applying for income support, and they also facilitate direct payment where income support is not being used for its intended purpose.

Mortgage lenders, however, felt that this reform did not go far enough, and pressed the Government to introduce mandatory direct payment in all cases. Clearly, the Government viewed this in a different light given the growing evidence about the depressed state of the mortgage market, and there was a significant change of policy towards the end of November. This led to the announcement, just before Christmas, that a Bill would shortly be introduced into Parliament to provide for direct payment of income support to mortgage lenders with effect from April of this year. Mortgage lenders believe that this will significantly reduce repossessions in the current year, and will also ensure that public money is used for its intended purpose.

'Mortgage Rescue Schemes'

The Government used the change of policy in respect of income support as a lever to push mortgage lenders to speed up the work which they had been doing on 'mortgage rescue schemes'. There is much misunderstanding about what mortgage rescue schemes can and cannot do. Some have the simplistic notion that merely transforming an owner-occupier into a tenant will reduce his housing costs. This cannot be the case. However, because the social security system provides generous benefit to low-income tenants, through housing benefit, but virtually no assistance to low-income owner-occupiers other than mortgage interest tax relief, transforming an owner-occupier into a tenant can significantly reduce his or her housing costs. However, even this is not sufficient. The mortgage rescue schemes that have worked in local authorities have done so only because of a substantial injection of public subsidy, perhaps £20,000 per case. It is hardly surprising that fewer than 100 people have been helped by such schemes.

Lenders have been considering schemes without additional government subsidy, as it has been made clear that no such subsidy will be forthcoming. Such schemes will, therefore, require to be financed on 'soft' terms by the lender. The flurry of meetings before Christmas led to announcements of various mortgage rescue schemes before lenders were really ready to launch them. Nevertheless, the announcement of a complete package was probably desirable. Lenders are now working out their schemes, generally in partnership with housing associations, and the details will be announced fairly shortly. Broadly speaking, however, mortgage rescue schemes have the following characteristics:

o They are designed to help people who have experienced a significant reduction in income, but with no entitlement to income support. They will be particularly appropriate where one partner has lost his job, or where the main breadwinner has lost a substantial proportion of his or her income.

o The properties will be either bought directly by the lender, or more commonly will be sold by the borrower to a housing association at an open-market valuation.

o If a housing association is purchasing the properties, then it will charge a rent in accordance with its normal rent policy. From this rent can be calculated the mortgage rate which can be serviced, and the lender and the housing association will then have to agree an appropriate rate of interest.

o In exchange for making a soft loan, and perhaps also writing off some of the debt, the lender will seek to recover its subsidy from any increase in the value of the property when it is eventually sold.

Broadly, for the lender, mortgage rescue schemes involve transforming a non-performing loan which could well lead to a substantial capital loss into a performing loan at a low rate of interest with probably a lower initial capital loss. The economics of it all are finely balanced, but there will, no doubt, be a significant revenue cost to lenders.

As part of the package, the Government threw in the temporary abolition of stamp duty on houses costing less than £250,000 until August 1992. This was possible only because of the further delay in introducing the Taurus system in the Stock Exchange, which has meant that the abolition of stamp duty on share transfers has been delayed. In itself, of course, the abolition of stamp duty is not going to make anyone buy a house, but in some cases it may be a factor tilting the balance, or encouraging people to bring forward the decision about a house purchase.

Effects of the Initiatives

No one pretends that the package of measures announced in December will dramatically change the housing market from severe depression to a very active market. All of these measures can influence activity only at the margin, but then so often it is the margin which determines what happens to the market. Lenders believe that as a result of this package of measures, the number of repossessions in 1992 will be sharply reduced from what it would otherwise have been. It might also be noted that the recent flurry of activity has had its desired effect of causing lenders to re-examine their procedures for handling arrears and repossessions generally, and also, hopefully, warning people that they should not do as so many are currently doing, that is, abandon the property. If all of the publicity can encourage people

61

facing mortgage arrears to contact their lender at the earliest possible opportunity, and if lenders are better equipped to help people through their difficulties, then these factors could have a bigger impact on arrears and repossessions than the more glamorous mortgage rescue schemes.

Conclusion: Possible Policy Measures

It is tempting to conclude this paper by considering what other measures the Government could take to stimulate the housing market. There are two possible options given the general wish not to increase public expenditure. The first is to stimulate demand further by changing the tax relief system. A simple increase in the tax relief ceiling to, say, £60,000 would be very expensive, adding several billion pounds a year to government expenditure if it was applied also to existing loans. However, there might be the possibility of increasing the tax relief ceiling to, say, £50,000 or £60,000 for new loans only, but combining this with a limit to the period for which tax relief was available. It might be noted that this appears to be precisely the policy of the Labour Party which has said that it wishes to restructure the tax relief system so as to ensure that more relief is obtained in the early years. This could be applied for a limited period only, or perhaps it could be applied as part of a general reform of tax relief which could include, say, a temporary increase in the tax relief ceiling to £50,000 to go with the introduction of, say, a seven- or 10-year period for which tax relief was available.

The second option is to take steps which would increase the number of people moving out of the social rented sector and buying into the owner-occupied sector. The Housing Corporation in England has a programme called the 'tenants' incentive scheme', under which grants of up to £15,000 are paid to housing association tenants who purchase into the owner-occupied market. However, only about 4,000 transactions are likely to be financed in the coming year. Many local authorities have similar programmes. The simple advantage of such schemes is that they make available a new social rented property at about £15,000 rather than the £60,000 to £80,000 that it might cost to build one. It is, of course, important to ensure that the grant is not paid to people who would have moved out anyway. If a significant number of people could be encouraged to take advantage of such schemes, say, between 50,000 and 100,000, this would undoubtedly give a stimulus to the lower end of the market, and, therefore, to the whole market, while at the same time increasing the supply of accommodation available to housing associations and local authorities to meet priority housing needs.

The case for introducing either of these measures is not overwhelming, but they certainly merit serious consideration.

5

1992 –
A REAL OPPORTUNITY FOR
PRIVATE RENTED HOUSING?

David A. Coleman

Department of Applied Social Studies,
University of Oxford

The Year of Lost Illusions

1991 MAY GO DOWN as the year when the British finally started to give up their obsession with owner-occupation. Two remarkable things have happened. First, more.people than ever before (almost 100,000 households) came to grief in their attempt to achieve the great British ambition of home ownership. For them, the inflation hedge of ownership had turned into an impenetrable maze of debt. Even more significant than the tragedies themselves, they have been front page news for most of the year. Many people, including some who are far from being economically marginal, know someone who has been re-possessed. Consequently, it has become respectable to talk about premature owner-occupation and the merits of renting, ideas previously confined to the housing chattering classes.

The other development was more positive. For the first time in perhaps 50 years, we have statistical evidence that reports of the death of private renting were indeed premature. First results of the 1990 Private Renters' Survey (OPCS, 1991a) showed the expected continued terminal decline of old regulated tenancies, so the total number of all private tenancies declined. That should surprise no-one. But the interesting fact was the extraordinary growth in tenancies under the

1988 Housing Act—assured shorthold and assured, together totalling about 483,000, all created in 1989 and the first half of 1990. Less than 10,000 of these are Business Expansion Scheme (BES) based; the rest are unsubsidised, except possibly indirectly through housing benefit.

More Rational Housing Choice?

Does new fear and new opportunity add up to a more rational balance in housing choice, a more realistic re-assessment of the merits of ownership versus renting? Yes, but there is no denying that the underlying biases in the system favouring ownership remain in place. High house prices and rents in Britain are primarily due to the constraints on supply created by the planning system, and the excess demand for early ownership created by the rewards of the tax system. These are estimated to inflate house prices by between 4 and 40 per cent, and 15 per cent, respectively. They turn natural changes in demand into price hikes and crashes, because supply is insufficiently elastic (Muellbauer, 1990; Maclennan, Gibb *et al.*, 1991; Cheshire, Sheppard *et al.*, 1985).

General inflation always tends to favour ownership, the more so in the inflation-prone British economy to which the subsidising of house prices makes its own contribution. There is little prospect of any easing of planning controls in the near future, especially in the South East, except for so-called 'social housing' or in the New Economic Zones of East London where no-one, not even Essex Girl, wants to live. Concern for rural house-price protection and social exclusiveness, falsely dressed up as environmental concern to impress jittery MPs, will see to that.

The other stokers of the inflationary fire are, of course, the tax reliefs on mortgages and the freedom from capital gains on disposal. These remain absolutely unchanged, except for the slow erosion of the real value of the £30,000 limit. The building society trade is inclined to pooh-pooh this problem, pointing to the fall in value of the tax concession with lower tax rates and higher mortgages now often over the limit—for first-time buyers an average of £60,000, and for all advances £47,000. That still accounted for £8 billion of taxpayers' money each year, a subsidy of at least £1,000 to the average new mortgage holder—equivalent to a higher salary of over 5 per cent. As average house prices have been declining in recent months, the proportion of housing costs covered by this genteel subsidy has been rising, not falling. All the equipment required to stoke up the boiler again is therefore still in place.

What Has Renting Got To Do With It?

Renting helps avoid some of these problems. With an adequate supply of rented housing, households can defer ownership until their finances are more robust, and possibly consume less housing, at lower cost, in the meantime. In all Western societies private renting is *par excellence* the tenure for the mobile job seeker. Britain has the smallest private rented sector of any industrial country (Table 1). In Britain, private (unregulated) tenants are roughly 10 times more mobile than owner-occupiers and about 50 per cent more likely to be moving for job reasons (Minford, Peel *et al.*, 1987; Salt, 1991). Shortage of rented housing depresses mobility by up to 15 per cent and was the subject of endless complaints from the CBI and employers in the good old days when they used to recruit workers (CBI, 1988; Banham, 1990).

Elsewhere, renting is taken for granted as the obvious way of getting instant access to housing without lawyers, queues, bureaucrats or capital. The bottom end of the private market is where many of today's homeless used to live. Some of this may seem academic at the moment. House prices are still falling and even demand for rented accommodation is slackening off because there are fewer job movers. But let us take a longer-term look at some of the underlying changes in our society which may affect demand for housing.

People and Households

In the long run, all Europe is running out of people, or at least of Europeans. The way things are going, Britain, Sweden and France will be the ones to turn the lights out; deaths in Germany, Denmark and Italy have already exceeded births. Without immigration their population would be declining, or declining faster. That will not happen to us until 2030 or so (OPCS, 1991b). In the long run, therefore, stagnation or decline in the number of households will reduce demand for the personal ownership of housing by undermining its future value, even with tax reliefs. The writing is already on the wall for the axiomatic assumption that the owner-occupation of property is an asset, not a liability.

All population projections are always wrong. What matters is *how* wrong they are. In fact, all the people who are going to form households for the next 20 years have already been born. So we know the underlying demand in terms of new individuals. What we do not know is when they will choose to leave home, how they will choose to live together, how fast their elders will get divorced, how fast they will

TABLE 1

DISTRIBUTION OF TENURES IN INDUSTRIAL COUNTRIES
IN THE LATE 1980s

(*per cent of total*)

Country	Type of Tenure: Owner-occupied %	Rented: Private %	Social %	Municipal %
UK 1988	67	7	3	23
Austria 1988	50	——— 42 ———		
Belgium 1990	72	n.a.	n.a.	n.a.
Denmark 1988	52	20	15	4
France 1988	51	23	——— 18 ———	
Greece 1990	72	n.a.	n.a.	n.a.
W. Germany 1988	37	45	——— 18 ———	
Italy 1990	68	n.a.	n.a	n.a.
Netherlands 1988	43	14	35	7
Norway 1990	73	n.a.	n.a.	n.a.
Spain 1988	77	19	2	2
Sweden 1988	39	23	——— 34 ———	
Switzerland 1988	30	23	——— 44 ———	
Canada 1986	63	——— 37 ———		0
USA 1985	64	32	0	2
Japan 1988	61	n.a.	n.a.	n.a.

Note: 'Other tenures' excluded. Recent breakdowns of the rented sector not available for many countries, so totals may not sum to 100.

Sources: 'Fast Facts', *Roof*, January-February 1991, Table 1; for detailed sources (mostly UN ECE) see *Roof*. Data for specified years from Emms (1991); Statistics Canada: 'Household Facilities by Income and Other Characteristics', Newton (1991).

cohabit or remarry afterwards. These imponderables depend not only on the numbers of people and on their domestic preferences; both are themselves constrained by the supply of housing. For example, British young people leave home rather later on average than those on the Continent, and get married earlier. Both tendencies may, in part, be laid to the shortage of private rented accommodation.

Housing demand depends in part on what is happening in the national bedroom. Divorce threatens one marriage in three but has not been increasing much in recent years, partly because marriage is later and therefore less risky. Cohabitation continues to rise and partly replace marriage; that may tend to delay ownership. Almost one birth in three now occurs outside marriage, mostly to allegedly 'stable' cohabiting unions which in fact are anything but stable. Their more rapid break-up than marriages may put more pressure on renting, private and subsidised. The allocation system of subsidised housing, first in the council sector, then in housing associations which are replacing them, has been claimed to encourage these demographic differences and accelerate household formation. That is controversial, but the demographic differences between owner-occupiers and residents of social housing are among the biggest between any social groups. Expectation of life keeps going up and up, despite AIDS, and is one of several reasons why household projections for the late 1980s are bigger than previously expected.

The baby boom has bulged on into middle age. The numbers of married couple households are expected to grow only in the baby boom age-groups—from age 30 upwards—while numbers below that age will actually decline. The married couple projected population continues to shrink and the alternatives to increase. In all, the total of new households and therefore dwellings is expected to increase from 1991 to 2001 by 1,567,000 or almost 160,000 per year—a further increase of 520,000 over the 1985 estimates which were 600,000 more than the 1983 estimates (Table 2).

Successive estimates for the number of new households by 2001 have therefore increased by 1·1 million from 1983 to 1989 (Department of the Environment, 1991); that is equivalent to the population of Birmingham, or equivalent on the Heseltine scale to 100 Foxley Woods. These projections, of course, take for granted existing constraints on household formation—that is to say, they assume the perpetuation of existing planning restrictions and the complete success of British immigration control policy.

Implications for Future Demand for Private Renting

Future trends in the composition of households mean that demand is weakest in just those areas where owner-occupation has been strongest, that is, in married couples. The households which are growing most in numbers are those which have traditionally rented,

TABLE 2

COMPARISON OF 1983, 1985 AND 1989-BASED HOUSEHOLD PROJECTIONS FOR ENGLAND
IN 1991, 1996 AND 2001

(*thousands*)

Projection for year	1991			1996			2001		
Made in	1983	1985	1989	1983	1985	1989	1983	1985	1989
All households	18,661	18,903	19,036	19,223	19,617	19,910	19,481	20,083	20,603
Married couple	10,689	10,559	10,572	10,739	10,449	10,342	10,746	10,350	10,142
Lone parent	1,728	1,868	1,891	1,808	2,013	2,148	1,832	2,074	2,336
One person	4,971	5,099	5,093	5,390	5,691	5,756	5,653	6,184	6,354
Other	1,272	1,378	1,481	1,286	1,465	1,665	1,250	1,475	1,771
Private h'hold popn.	46,622	47,213	47,255	47,128	48,001	48,036	47,535	48,622	48,752
Mean household size	2·50	2·50	2·48	2·45	2·45	2·41	2·44	2·42	2·37

Sources: Department of the Environment (1986): 1983-based estimates of numbers of households in England, the Regions, Counties, Metropolitan Districts and London Boroughs, 1983-2001, London: HMSO, Table 2; Department of the Environment (1988): 1985-based estimates of numbers of households in England, the Regions, Counties, Metropolitan Districts and London Boroughs, 1985-2001, London: HMSO, Table 2; Department of the Environment (1991): *Household Projections, England 1989-2011*: 1989-based estimates of numbers of households for Regions, Counties, Metropolitan Districts and London Boroughs, London: HMSO, Table 1.

either at a subsidised rent or through private landlords, although the slow increase in the population's average age is moving it slightly away from the younger age-groups where renting is more common. Divorce has always been the quickest route from owner-occupation to the council estate, and over 150,000 are divorced each year. Each divorce creates about 1·5 new households where there was one before. The ratio is worsening as remarriage rates decline. Single (unmarried) mothers often go straight into local authority accommodation through the priority given under the homelessness legislation.

Private Renting Today: the 1988 and 1990 Private Renters' Surveys

The 1988 and 1990 Private Renters'Surveys (OPCS, 1991a; Dodd, 1990) have thrown new light on renting. The 1988 survey, made at the nadir of renting, before the 1988 Housing Act had come into effect, showed that most private tenants were satisfied with their accommodation. Some people in private renting had come from ownership, most of the younger tenants were intending to become owners, a high proportion had taken the tenancy in relation to work. In the newer, unregulated sector young flat sharers predominated. The 1988 Act created two new kinds of tenancy: new assured tenancies with market rents but fairly tight security, and assured shortholds with market rents subject to scrutiny and six months' minimum let followed by renewal. To avoid trying to kick-start the initiative uphill, as it were, the second essential prerequisite—of a subsidy—was provided through an extension of the BES scheme. All this was launched under the variable hostility, depending on which spokesperson was speaking, of the Labour Party. What has happened over two years?

The decline of the old rented sector, beyond the reach of the rent reform, continues as the tenants die off or move to nursing homes, and the thankful landlords (including a few remaining institutions) sell their houses and quit renting for ever. Registered tenancies with regulated rent have gone down from 444,000 in 1988 to 313,000 in 1990 (a 30 per cent decline) and the 568,000 regulated without registered rent to 258,000 (a decline of 310,000 or 55 per cent). Most of the former were old tenancies to old people. Most of the latter would have been informal tenancies, some quite short term. Part of the reason for their collapse is that none can have been created since 1988 (Table 3).

By contrast, there has been an extraordinary increase in the new tenancies which did not exist before the Housing Act came into force in January 1989. By mid-1990 there were 136,000 assured shorthold

71

TABLE 3

TYPES OF PRIVATE LETTINGS IN 1988 AND 1990

Types of letting	1988		1990		Change 1988-1990	
	thousands	per cent	thousands	per cent	thousands	per cent
Resident landlord	102	5·9	68	4·0	-34	-33·3
No security	68	3·9	78	4·6	10	14·7
Not accessible to public:						
rented	233	13·4	218	12·9	-15	-6·4
rent free	253	14·5	242	14·3	-11	-4·3
Regulated, registered rent	444	25·5	313	18·5	-131	-29·5
Regulated, no registered rent	568	32·6	258	15·2	-310	-54·6
Protected shorthold and pre-1989 assured	72	4·1	35	2·1	-37	-51·4
Assured shorthold	0	0·0	136	8·0	136	
Post-1988 assured	0	0·0	347	20·5	347	
Total	1,740	100·0	1,695	100·0	-45	-2·6

Source: OPCS (1991a), Table 2.

tenancies and 347,000 shorthold, all created after January 1989 (483,000 in all). This just compensates for the decline in regulated tenancies, but they were different tenancies to different people. Regulated tenancies existing before 1988 cannot be turned into the new tenancies. As it was tenants who were interviewed, not landlords, the answers can probably be relied on.

The surveys confirm the view that private renting is mostly short-term, and that tenants are younger than average. Most private tenancies are adults only, with relatively few families with children. Private rents do not seem to be very high. Overall, in 1990 the mean rent, excluding services, was £43 per week (£30 in 1988). This compares with about £27 for council and housing association rents. These average rents do not mean much because they combine regulated and market rents. Regulated tenancies with registered rent averaged £27. Post-1988 assured rents were £61; and assured shorthold rents £66. Even though higher than the average of £43, they are less than the £86 per week average first net mortgage instalment in 1990 (Housing Finance No. 11), although they also buy less housing, often of a lower quality.

Other Evidence for the Revival of Supply and Demand for Renting

The results of the BES scheme are also encouraging. BES was extended to housing as a belated recognition that deregulation was only half the answer to reviving renting; it also needed a more equal tax treatment with ownership. BES attracted £461 million into 188 BES companies for private renting from 1988 to April 1990, and by September 1991 was estimated to have attracted £800 million in all. The former figure is equivalent to about 9,000 dwellings, the latter (assuming £50,000 per dwelling) to 16,000. Only a fifth of companies failed to attract the minimum investment (usually £500,000), despite the risks. Most of the dwellings were new purpose-built flats or 1900s terraced houses which would not otherwise have been made available for renting (Crook, Kemp *et al.*, 1991; Villiers, 1992).

That number is still equivalent only to the council holdings of the average council. But it shows there is faith in the demand for rented housing, as well as in its durable capital value even when let. None of the schemes can mature after the next election, thus risking their maturity under a Labour Party which, despite endless relaunches of policy and backing and filling on renting, has strong prejudices against the private sector, as revealed in its latest double-decker plan for renting; and it has promised the abolition of the BES scheme.

Success of BES Schemes

An excellent study of BES (Crook, Kemp *et al.*, 1991, p. 7) concludes rather grudgingly that

> 'if the Government had channelled the same amount of money (£202-225m) into housing association development, the number of rented dwellings produced would have been at least 3/5ths of the number produced through the BES'.

I would prefer to say that the BES scheme produced 40 per cent more new rented dwellings than housing associations could have done with the same money.

An encouraging sign is the speed at which the properties have been snapped up by a wide range of tenants of a most varied range of origins, underlining a substantial and hitherto unmet demand. BES was targeted at 'professionals' in a broad sense and students; only a few schemes were directed at retired people or at people on middle to low incomes. Tenants had high satisfaction with their new homes (75 per cent) compared with previous rented homes (28 per cent), indicating the effects of competition in attracting tenants away from unsatisfactory landlords. Two-thirds were in full or part-time work; a third of them were professionals, employers or managers, and 28 per cent were in manual jobs. Although 30 per cent earned £20,000 a year or over, 28 per cent had less than £8,000 and a quarter of households were receiving benefits, mostly in the North and North West. A third had moved three times or more in the last three years, mostly for job reasons. Thirty-eight per cent of the likely movers intended to become owner-occupiers, and 29 per cent expected to move on for job or study reasons. A third had considered buying before their move into a BES tenancy; most decided they could not afford it. Half of those who had not seriously considered buying had dismissed the idea because of the cost.

Further indications of vigorous demand for renting come from the Association of Residential Letting Agents, who reported an approximately 60 per cent increase from 1989 up to the beginning of the current depression, and from the performance of Quality Street, the first new national rented housing company. Despite the absence of subsidy, but with backing from a building society, it has grown from zero to 2,000 rented dwellings since 1987, 95 per cent of them newly built, and maintains an occupancy rate of between 92 and 96 per cent. So renting is a way to a job for some, and a way out of the problems of affordability of ownership for others, providing homes for ordinary people, not dependent on the state, who are excluded by the rules of 'social housing'.

Time for a Radical Change?

The time seems right for a change. Faith in owner-occupation as a safe haven has taken a hammering from repossessions. Premature occupation is now seen as a vice, not something in which Britain should be glad to lead the world. The fiscal lunacy of progressive tax reliefs for occupation, long realised by almost everyone, has been brought into prominence by the inflationary effects of equity withdrawal. That is estimated to have been £30 billion in 1988 compared with £0·9 billion in 1970 (Holmans, 1991), and may have added 3 per cent to national spending power (Maclennan, Gibb *et al.*, 1991). The renewed necessity to fight inflation now has a European dimension—the realisation that the house inflation system is likely to compromise our position in the ERM by making national inflation that much more difficult to control (Muellbauer, 1990). We can no longer continue to run two inflation systems: national inflation bad, to be squeezed out of the system; house-price inflation good, at least for votes, subsidised by tax breaks capitalised into price and encouraging everyone to jump on the inflationary spiral as soon as they cannot afford it!

What Is To Be Done?

The abolition or modification of tax breaks on owner-occupation would be the first priority. But no-one has yet succeeded in persuading politicians that such statements would not constitute a suicide note. That being so, a replacement for BES, which is due to end next year, is a priority. It should be directed more to encouraging institutions to move into renting. The aims would be to:

o persuade BES companies or their private successors to carry on renting;

o encourage large institutions as well as 40 per cent taxpayers to invest directly, perhaps with the management hired out to housing associations;

o involve ordinary small savers, to increase finance and even more important to help rehabilitate renting as an everyday service for instant housing.

The tradition in British housing reform is always to take the path of least resistance—to build on existing ideas or institutions. The easiest reform would be to extend tax advantages to institutions to make rented housing a more natural part of their portfolio. There are several existing ways of achieving this end:

o Re-introduce capital allowances for building or acquisition for renting. When that was tried in the early 1980s it created a brief flurry of investment, despite positive vetting for landlords and other restrictions, until a whimsical Treasury snuffed it out again. Today allowances are restricted to industrial buildings, permitting 4 per cent of their capital costs per year to be written down against tax from income over 25 years, or 25 per cent on a reducing-balance basis for certain capital goods.

o Sideways relief: allowing losses in some parts of an enterprise to be set against profits elsewhere is another conventional business practice which should be extended to renting. That would involve treating renting as trading, not investment, as furnished lettings used to be. At present it applies only to furnished holiday lets—a strange recipient for public largesse from the viewpoint of housing policy.

Neither of these is ideal. Sideways relief benefits existing traders, but gives no special incentive to new investors, who are so badly needed. It is good to encourage existing institutions with varied interests to add renting to them, not so good that the attractions depend on the vagaries of making a loss somewhere else—not too difficult these days, of course. The capital allowance system also gives no added incentive for the risk element still perceived in renting innovation; nor does it help with the high front-end loading involved in building housing for rent from scratch.

Incentives for Institutional Investment in Renting

o One way of giving a kick-start to renting by institutions might be to give enhanced allowances—perhaps 10 per cent for the first five years over the following five years—to new renting schemes by companies and institutions.

○ Another route is to involve the public sector. That would have the important additional advantage of extending the reach of private or partly-private renting to households which otherwise might think 'council' and nothing but 'council', with its built-in labour immobility and other problems. Two obvious ways of doing this already exist or need only minor adjustments.

○ Section 28 of the Local Government Act, 1988, allows local authorities to give capital grants to investors in private housing. It has been little taken up. Some local authorities detest the idea of private landlords. More generally, the grant competes with other council funds. However, if councils were allowed to draw on capital receipts for this purpose, perhaps with some nomination rights in exchange, the scheme might take off, especially if institutions were to be targeted.

○ The Housing Corporation is a quango whose function is to promote, fund and regulate housing associations. Under the Housing Associations Act, 1985, it can give grants only to registered housing associations. A small change in the law would enable it to give grants under similar terms to approved private institutions. That would introduce a real choice in housing for middle income and poorer tenants, and challenge the monopoly currently enjoyed by housing associations. These institutions are growing to resemble local authority housing departments. Many are being created directly overnight through voluntary transfers of whole housing departments and thereby acquiring a near-monopoly of housing the poor in some areas, just as councils once did (Coleman, 1990).

All of these innovations should be tried, subject perhaps to an overall limit of tax relief from all sources. In Britain we are too prone to find one solution and apply it globally. The Americans, with a much bigger and more varied sector than ours, experiment with many kinds of tax incentives and subsidies. If savings are needed, they should be made by nibbling at the edges of mortgage/income tax relief.

All these suggestions are intended to help the supply side. While consumer subsidies will filter through to producers eventually, they will also serve to push up price when supply is limited (in Britain) through the planning system, as Professor Alan Evans explains in the next paper in this volume.

Inducements for Small Savers?

One final proposal is to involve more savers. The absence of a tradeable rented housing bond is often thought to be an impediment in creating a new rented market. The incentives above could raise returns on renting sufficiently to make it viable for institutional investment. But to put owning on a level field with renting also means involving the small saver in it, just as the small saver, irrespective of the tenure of his home, is involved in ownership through the building societies. The larger renting institutions (those approved by a reformed Housing Corporation and receiving the equivalent of Housing Association Grant) might combine with some of the progressive housing associations to pay dividends on small investments in rented housing, regulated as the building societies are now. If returns were not competitive to begin with, then a short-term housing TESSA might be introduced whereby basic rate tax were removed from such investments for five years.

The aim is to make access to rented housing as easy and commonplace as it is in the USA and on the Continent, and to create in rented housing the same kind of supermarket approach we have for our other needs. Preference for owner-occupation should depend on its housing advantages, not an imperative inflation hedge which is so huge that it helps create the inflation it is meant to protect against. A viable rented sector is a natural complement to ownership, not a challenge to it, and its two- or three-fold growth would be quite compatible with 80 per cent or more of households eventually owning their homes after a longer period of renting.

Conclusion

In these, as in other respects, Britain is likely to converge on Europe and the rest of the industrial world. We all know that seriously rich countries in Europe do not share our obsession with owning homes. As our financial systems and inflation rates are affected more by Europe, housing systems too may converge, not the least because foreign letting companies may see openings here. We already have French-run private water companies, so perhaps the concierge is coming too, together with the benefits of private apartment living in city centres which make inner-city life so much more pleasant in

Continental provincial cities than in our own. On the Continent there is much to copy; private renting is not so rigidly separated from subsidised renting, and for the most part they have avoided our disastrous council renting system. Ownership is also growing in Europe, since their ownership system is under-developed. We are moving to the same position from the other extreme, both in terms of a rational balance between renting and owning, and of a rational mixture of private and public money.

REFERENCES

Banham, J. (1990): 'CBI Demands Rethink on Housing Policy', *Housing Choice*, 2, pp. 1-2.

Cheshire, P. C., S. Sheppard, *et al.* (1985): *The Economic Consequences of the British Planning System: Some Empirical Results*, Reading: Department of Economics, University of Reading.

Coleman, D. A. (1990): 'The New Housing Policy: A Critique', *Housing Studies*, Vol. 4, No. 1, pp. 44-57.

Confederation of British Industry (1988): 'Companies and the Housing Market', *CBI News*, March 1988.

Confederation of British Industry (1991): 'The Cost of Relocation', *Relocation News*, No. 17, pp. 3-17.

Crook, A., P. Kemp, *et al.* (1991): *The Business Expansion Scheme and Rented Housing*, York: Joseph Rowntree Foundation.

Department of the Environment (1991): *Household Projections: England 1989-2011*, London: HMSO.

Dodd, T. (1990): *Private Renting in 1988. The Report of a Survey Carried Out by the Social Survey Division of OPCS on Behalf of the Department of the Environment*, London: HMSO.

Emms, P. (1991): *Social Housing: A European Dilemma*, Bristol: School of Advanced Urban Studies, Bristol University.

Holmans, A. E. (1991): *Estimates of Housing Equity Withdrawal by*

Owner Occupiers in the United Kingdom 1970 to 1990, London: Department of the Environment.

Maclennan, D., K. Gibb, *et al.* (1991): *Fairer Subsidies, Faster Growth*, York: Joseph Rowntree Foundation.

Minford, P., M. Peel, and P. Ashton (1987): *The Housing Morass: Regulation, Immobility and Unemployment*, Hobart Paperback No. 25, London: Institute of Economic Affairs.

Muellbauer, J. (1990): *The Great British Housing Disaster*, London: Institute for Public Policy Research.

Newton, J. (1991): *All In One Place*, London: Catholic Housing Aid Society.

OPCS (1991a): *The 1990 Private Renters' Survey: Preliminary Results*, Monitor SS 91/2, London: OPCS.

OPCS (1991b): *1989-Based National Population Projections*, London: HMSO.

Salt, J. (1991): 'Labour Migration and Housing in the UK: An Overview', in J. Allen and C. Hamnett (eds.), *Housing and Labour Markets*, London: Unwin Hyman.

Villiers, T. (1992): Personal communication from the BES Association, London.

6

TOWN PLANNING AND THE SUPPLY OF HOUSING

Alan W. Evans

University of Reading

Introduction

WHEN I WAS ASKED to contribute a paper to the IEA's third *State of the Economy* colloquium, it was suggested that I could discuss the costs of the British system of town and country planning.

Shortly afterwards housing came to the fore as a major policy problem, the subject of newspaper headlines and government initiatives. Now repossessions and falling prices seem initially to have little to do with a system which by limiting land availability, raises prices. Nevertheless, paradoxical though it might appear, I shall show that they are connected.

Why should housing be a problem in this country? Why should there be a shortage of housing? Why should the ownership of housing be regarded as desirable to the extent that the private rented sector has virtually disappeared? And why should the price of housing vary so much over the cycle?

Although of course there are several factors which are involved in any of these policy problems, an underlying factor is the operation of the British planning system. The pervasiveness of its economic effects are perhaps equalled by the almost total ignorance of these effects amongst economists and economic commentators—an ignorance

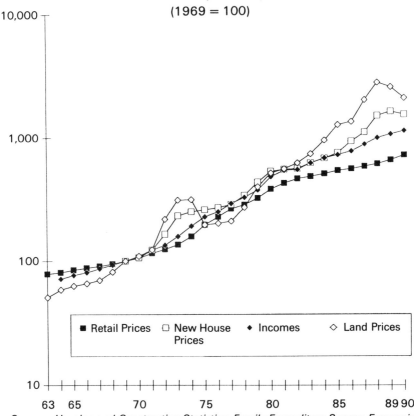

Figure 1: New House Prices, Housing Land Prices and Incomes in the South East (Outside Greater London) and Retail Prices (National), 1963-90

$(1969 = 100)$

Legend: ■ Retail Prices ☐ New House Prices ◆ Incomes ◇ Land Prices

Sources: *Housing and Construction Statistics; Family Expenditure Survey; Economic Trends.*

which is understandable given that most economics courses in this country would regard one lecture on the theory of land rent some time in the first year as all that any professional economist needs to know on the subject of land and location, but unforgivable, in my view, given its economic importance.

The Statistical Background

Before we consider the way in which the planning system operates, we should first look at the evidence regarding the price of housing in

TABLE 1

WEIGHTED AND UNWEIGHTED HOUSE PRICE INDICES:
REST OF SOUTH EAST ENGLAND (1975 = 100)

Year	Unweighted	Weighted
1975	100	100
1976	106	107
1977	112	114
1978	129	133
1979	168	177
1980	203	214
1981	204	224
1982	202	226
1983	230	256
1984	255	290
1985	276	320
1986	331	378
1987	391	461
1988	495	598
1989	557	691
1990	549	634

Britain. Figure 1 shows indices of the average price of housing and of housing land in South East England over the last 30 years as well as indices of the incomes of households in that region and of (national) retail prices. It can easily be seen that land values have increased astronomically and that house prices have risen much faster than retail prices in general. They also appear not to have risen much faster than incomes but this is misleading—the index of house prices used here, and the one most often used in this kind of analysis, is an index of the average price of houses bought and sold. But it will be appreciated that the amount people are willing to pay for a house is largely dependent on their income, not on the price of housing. If the price of housing goes up, they will spend the same amount of money but they will buy a smaller house. Thus we should expect to find what the figures show— the average amount people spend on their housing generally rises in

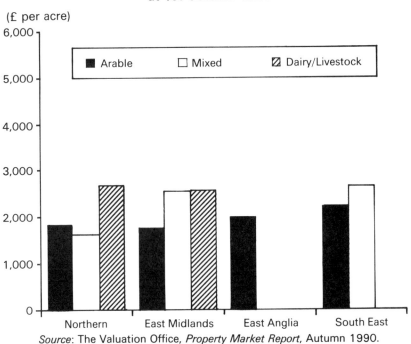

**Figure 2:   Values of Agricultural Land with Vacant Possession
at 1st October 1990**

(£ per acre)

Source: The Valuation Office, *Property Market Report*, Autumn 1990.

line with their incomes, although they may be willing to spend more in
boom years when prices are rising and the future looks rosy, but cut
back in recession years when house prices are not rising and future
income increases are more uncertain.

A truer index of house prices is set out in column 2 of Table 1. This
shows the average price of a standard housing mix and can be compared
with the average amount people spend on housing, the index portrayed
in Figure 1, which is set out in column 1. The comparison reveals
something else. It shows that as the price of housing has risen over the
period people have responded in the way an economist would expect
by buying less housing than they otherwise would have done.

One further piece of evidence is necessary and that is set out in
Figure 2 which shows the price of agricultural land in a number of
areas along the eastern side of England, and in Figure 3 which shows
the price of land with planning permission for residential development
outside towns in this part of the country. The difference in scales

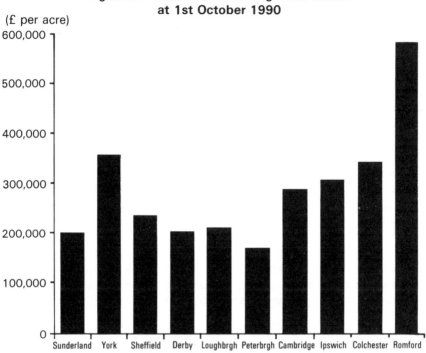

Figure 3: Residential Building Land Values at 1st October 1990

Source: The Valuation Office, *Property Market Report*, Autumn 1990.

should be noted—the one is one hundred times that of the other. So the award of planning permission can raise the price of land a hundredfold or more, clear evidence that the supply of land for housing is restricted by the planning system, so that the high price of housing is a consequence of that restrictiveness and of the failure to increase the supply of land over the years as the demand for housing has increased in line with incomes and with the growth in the number of households.

Town Planning System: Some Background

Most people fail to realise just how restrictive is the town planning system. Virtually everybody is aware that London is surrounded by a Green Belt. Somewhat fewer are aware that this is true of most major cities and historic towns. And virtually everybody I have ever met believes that these green belts are, and should remain, sacrosanct.

Most believe, however, that that is the end of the matter so that when I argue that the planning system restricts the supply of land I am usually told that this means that I want to build all over the green belts. To clear this up I should here state that I agree with the principle of green belts as a foundation for good city planning.

There is, however, a case for saying that they are too extensive. At the present time the area of England which is designated as green belt is about as large as that covered by urban development—about 11 per cent of the total land area in each case (Elson, 1986). This would represent no problem if there were not further restrictions covering the remaining parts of the country. The most important of these are the Areas of Outstanding Natural Beauty. In southern England these include the Chilterns, the Wessex Downs, the Surrey Hills, and so on. Any developer knows that permission is unlikely to be obtained for any major, or even any minor, proposal for development in these areas.

Local politicians are aware that development is unpopular with their current electorate and so in structure plans in all rural areas, policies are devised to try to prevent development. For example, in the Explanatory Memorandum to the Oxfordshire Structure Plan Proposed Alterations No. 4, policy H1 states that

'The principal locations for new housing will be in the country towns of Banbury, Bicester, Didcot and Witney where they can be conveniently served by public transport. Elsewhere a policy of general restraint will apply.'

Usually such a policy of general restraint is buttressed by a number of other policies. Table 2 lists relevant policies drawn from the structure plans of the Counties of Oxfordshire, Berkshire, Hampshire, Surrey, and Buckinghamshire. Although it is perhaps somewhat unfair to draw policies from a number of different plans, Table 2 vividly conveys the message that, although land outside urban areas might be thought of by most people as available for development, there will invariably be some policy which can be brought forward to be cited as a bar to any proposal, even if that policy is merely one of 'general restraint'.

The result has been that the supply of housing land has been increasingly restricted. In economic jargon, the price elasticity of the supply of land for housing and of housing itself has been low. A recent study by Tsoukis and Westaway (1991) of the NIESR suggested that the long-run elasticity of housing supply in Britain is about one. As

TABLE 2

LAND NOT AVAILABLE FOR HOUSING: A TYPOLOGY

General	*Heritage, natural history and countryside*
1. Developed land including transport land	17. Agricultural, horticultural and forestry land
2. Land scheduled for other uses	18. Local nature reserves
3. Presumptions against development outside of the existing built up areas except for infill, rounding off and redevelopment	19. Other sites of natural importance
	20. Historic parks and gardens
	21. Archaeological sites
4. No coalescence of sporadic or dispersed settlements	22. Landscape features
	23. National Trust land
Statutorily designated areas	24. Specific river valleys, canals, etc.
5. Green belt	*Miscellaneous*
6. Areas of outstanding natural beauty (AONBS)	25. Public recreation land
7. Sites of special scientific interest (SSSIs)	26. Mineral workings and commitments
	27. Polluted land
8. National nature reserves	28. Waste disposal sites
9. Common land	29. Areas liable to flood
Locally designated areas	30. Water safeguarding areas
10. Areas beyond the green belt	31. Air safeguarding areas
11. Areas of great landscape value	*Government land*
12. Areas of high ecological importance	32. Ministry of Defence land
13. Settlements and their setting	33. Crown land
14. Gaps between settlements	
15. Green corridors and spaces	
16. Areas of urban landscape quality	

they remark, 'this contrasts sharply with Topel and Rosen's (1988) estimates from US data of a very high long-run elasticity whose order is between 2 and 24'. In other words, a 1 per cent increase in price will bring about a 1 per cent increase in the amount of housing available in the UK after a year or so but an increase of between 2 and 24 per cent in the USA.

The effect of this inelasticity has been that increases in the demand for housing, as incomes have increased and the number of households has risen, have largely resulted in increases in the amount of available housing in the USA but in increases in the price of housing in the UK.

Consequences—Short Run

One consequence of the relatively low elasticity of supply of housing in the UK is that price fluctuations are much more violent than they otherwise would be. As the demand for housing increases at the beginning of any upturn in the economy, so the price of housing increases for, in the very short run, the supply is virtually fixed. In other countries this increase in price would result in a substantial increase in the supply of housing so that further increases in demand would not result in the same price increases—the increase in demand would be balanced by the increase in supply. In Britain, however, the supply response is slow and delayed by the lengthy processes of obtaining planning permission. These may include negotiations with the planning officers before an application is made, waiting on the result of the application, and then possibly going to appeal and waiting on the result of the appeal, then possibly making a revised application, and so on.

So, as we saw in the mid-1980s, rapid house price escalation can be accompanied by frenzied activity on the part of developers seeking planning permission but only by relatively small increases in the amount of housing being built. Thus, between 1980 and 1990 the average price of dwellings mortgaged by the building societies rose from £24,300 to £66,700—that is, by 170 per cent. But during the same period total house completions in the UK rose by only 30 per cent from a low of 175,800 in 1982 to reach 229,200 in 1988, falling back again to 186,900 in 1990.[1]

In 1990 and 1991, what we have seen, of course, is falling house prices; indeed, prices would have fallen further and faster if the property market were not a highly imperfect market, one where would-be sellers have been unwilling to sell at prices lower than they can either afford or feel entitled to receive. So we have seen repossessions as well as vacant properties and falling prices. Because the supply is inelastic, prices rose but the quantity of housing supplied did not rise to the

---

[1] *Source*: DoE Housing and Construction Statistics.

extent that it would have done in other countries. As demand fell when interest rates were increased, so prices also fell, and they had further to fall because of the previous dramatic rise.

What we see is the hangover after the party is over—and almost as inevitable. 'Almost' because at the end of the house price booms of the early and late 1970s the problems in the housing market seemed less pressing. But this was only because of large doses of what one might call the 'hair of the dog'. The two house price inflations of the 1970s were followed by two periods of general price inflation. House prices therefore fell substantially in real terms but they did not fall in money terms. So the housing market was less dislocated and forced sellers usually did not have to sell at a loss. Paradoxically, therefore, the Government's success in reducing inflation is one cause of the current problems in the housing market.

Consequences—Long Run

For most of the population these wild swings in the housing market are unimportant. They are of urgent importance to those who bought at or near the top of the market, who borrowed a very high proportion of the purchase price, and whose income has fallen since then. (A substantial proportion of this group is likely to be made up of those unmarried couples encouraged to buy at the top of the market by Nigel Lawson's announcement that mortgage interest tax relief for this group would be reduced at the end of July 1988.)

For the vast majority, the important thing is that house prices have increased over the last 40 or so years. There have been fluctuations, it is true, but only in the last two years have there actually been widespread falls in house prices.

The importance of this general long-run increase in the price of housing is that it has been a major factor in encouraging the British population to buy their homes instead of renting. Those who have bought have found that they have purchased an asset which has substantially increased in value. Moreover, the purchase has almost always been financed by a substantial loan equal to (say) 90 per cent of the original cost, so that the gearing has been substantial. For example, anyone buying a house in 1980 for £100,000 and borrowing £90,000 would have seen their property rise in price to about £270,000 10 years later and the value of their initial investment increase from £10,000 to £180,000. Because of this most home owners have seen an increase in their apparent wealth which could not have been achieved in any other way, and the price falls of the past year or so have merely reduced their paper profits.

These apparent profits have tended to distort the working of the British economy in a number of ways. The first is to encourage home ownership, and to assist in the virtual elimination of the private rented sector. I am aware that governments have seen the growth of owner-occupation as something to be encouraged, but I would argue that the *costs* of owner-occupation seem to have been neglected. In the first place, owner-occupation reduces mobility. It is economically efficient for young people to rent housing before they are settled, so that they can move easily. Owner-occupation, almost as much as local authority housing, discourages mobility and slows down the adjustment and growth of the economy. In the second place, house purchase, just as much as share purchase, should come with a warning that prices may fall as well as rise. A combination of factors, which we have already discussed, has caused this possibility to be neglected, so that when prices have eventually fallen people have been hurt who could not afford to be.

Another way in which the long-run increase in house prices has tended to distort the economy is related to this last point. People have come to see home ownership as an investment or speculation—not something which is owned because it provides housing services but something which is primarily owned because of the capital gains which are expected to accrue and have accrued from its ownership. Because of this people are less likely to save and less likely to invest in British industry. For most people the increases in the value of their home have been far greater than the amounts they could save out of income. So why save? And why not buy a larger house than is required in order to maximise these gains? So saving in Britain is less than it would be and investment in British industry is less.

Finally, one should point to the fact that because the supply of land has been restricted in all parts of the country, the price of land for development has risen more in the South where the demand has been greatest and less in other parts of the UK. Migration from the North to the South has been discouraged by the high house prices ruling in the South, and this has helped to slow down growth in the country as a whole. It is also probable that the increases in house prices have helped to fuel wage demands, particularly in the South, and so to fuel the inflationary spiral in post-war Britain.

Planning and the Single Market

So what is the relevance of this to the operation of the Single European Market? It is relevant because none of our European partners operates planning systems which are half as stringent as that operating in Britain. As a result, the cost of land for any urban development is far higher in Britain than elsewhere. In other words, we operate at a self-imposed cost disadvantage. Anyone seeking confirmation of this need do no more than to ask those people who now own second homes in France rather than this country, or to look in the property pages of *The Sunday Times*. You will discover that prices there seem to be at most half what you might pay here. A consequence then of our stringent planning system is that we are importing housing services from France which might have been produced here.

Further, because the cost of housing is higher in England than in Europe, and because housing represents a large proportion of total living costs, the standard of living of British households would be lower than the standard across the Channel even if wages and other costs were the same. The long-run neo-classical market solution would be for much of the British population to migrate across the Channel until the population adjusted to the land allocated for its occupation. Some migration will occur—the purchase of second homes is a harbinger of this, for many will eventually become first homes—but the continuing prospect is for a lower standard of living in Britain.

The movement towards a single currency will also affect, and be affected by, the housing market and the planning system. The tendency will be to move towards uniformity in inflation rates and interest rates. But in the UK over the past 30 years or so housing has risen in price faster than most other goods because demand has exceeded supply, and housing accounts for a high proportion of total household expenditure. Either, therefore, the rate of increase in house prices falls to European levels or the rate of increase of other prices will have to be lower than elsewhere with a consequent continuing deflationary impact. If the supply of housing land is not increased, it follows that either the demand for housing is held down or the demand for other goods.

Other problems and processes of adjustment are not discussed here because they involve land uses other than housing, but they should perhaps be mentioned. Restrictions on the supply of land mean that the price of all land for urban uses is considerably higher than elsewhere. As a result, manufacturing, wholesaling, and commercial uses are also at a disadvantage relative to the rest of Europe, particularly those located in southern England where land prices are highest. This discourages the location of these activities here, particularly those such as manufacturing which use large amounts of land relative to capital and labour, and encourages the location of growing firms elsewhere in Europe.

Conclusion

It may be thought that I exaggerate the economic importance of the planning system. I personally find it surprising that, when economists seek reasons for the slow growth of the British economy since 1945, none has paid attention to the planning system set up in 1947—a system which, unlike other factors which they have examined, deliberately sets out to restrain growth. For example, the Oxfordshire Structure Plan Amendments mentioned earlier state that the county 'does not wish to restrict unduly the development of small firms, or the expansion of firms', which actually means that they *do* wish to restrict the growth of firms. But how much is 'not . . . unduly'? One per cent per annum? That does not sound very much but in the context of economic growth it is a very substantial amount. Moreover, people can be proud of their achievement in restraining development and slowing economic growth. An item in the *Reading Chronicle* (12 May 1989) reported the councillor who had been chairman of the Borough's planning committee for the previous three years as saying that 'he thought the committee had achieved a considerable amount over the last three years'. But what were these achievements?

> 'Not one new major office development has been approved in Reading that was not already in the pipeline when we took over. We managed to keep development down.'

There is an inherent conflict between land use and development which neither British governments nor the British people have understood. This is particularly evident in the case of housing. We have numerous fiscal policies which are designed to encourage people to spend more on housing and hence to buy larger houses—mortgage interest tax relief, the abolition of a tax on the imputed income from housing (the old Schedule A), no VAT on new dwellings, no capital gains tax on first homes, the abolition of the rates. Yet we have physical policies designed to restrict the amount of land available for housing. Separately they make sense, together they are a nonsense.

The effect of the restraints on land supply is to ensure that the fiscal benefits are translated into higher land prices and higher house prices.

Either the fiscal incentives have to be reduced and eliminated or the restraints on land supply have to be relaxed.

REFERENCES

Elson, Martin J. (1986): *Green Belts*, London: Heinemann.

Topel, R., and S. Rosen (1988): 'Housing Investment in the United States', *Journal of Political Economy*, Vol. 96, No. 4, pp. 718-40.

Tsoukis, C., and P. Westaway (1991): *A Forward Looking Model of Housing Construction in the UK*, Unpublished paper, London: National Institute of Economic and Social Research.

7

BETTER NEWS FROM THE TRENCHES: THE UK LABOUR MARKET AND THE SUPPLY SIDE

Patrick Minford

Edward Gonner Professor of Applied Economics, University of Liverpool

Introduction: Preserve the Gains from Recession

Dᴇᴘʀᴇssᴇᴅ AS the economy is by the Government's total incompetence in managing demand, its 'supply side'—that is, its long-term capacity to produce—is in remarkable shape underneath the shambles. When eventually the hammer blows from Mr Major and his bovver boys have stopped raining down on it, the economy should therefore do quite well again after convalescence.

It was the Austrian economist Joseph Schumpeter who remarked, in a not overly friendly way—he was something of a socialist—that capitalist recessions were 'gales of creative destruction'. He meant that recessions led to re-organisation of and within firms, new attitudes among workers, unions and managements: in today's terms they become 'leaner and meaner' and better at screwing more value-added out of their inputs. After all, those business failures and repossessions do not mean that physical assets are destroyed; the plants, the factories and the houses are still there and, if worth using, will find new owners more capable or less burdened with debt.

However, there is a proviso: that government does not step in to bail out the dispossessed. If it does, then the incentive to re-organise is blunted and may disappear completely. The BLs that are 'taken over' by a National Enterprise Board, just like the unemployed that are offered indefinite support on the dole, become the walking wounded of the next decade, a burden on themselves and everyone else.

That is why recessions are a two-edged instrument, particularly if interest groups are powerful and the people tender-hearted. Instead of being creative, the recessional destruction can too easily become a source of permanent invalidity. So far in this recession there has been only a limited resort to subsidy and intervention, of which the most blatant has been the mortgage and repossession scheme forced on the building societies. If the Labour Party wins the General Election it could be another story altogether.

But so far this Government has on the whole resisted the strong 'Fixit' tendency within it. Hence the recession, while dangerous and wasteful in the short term, should at least not damage the painfully-won gains in efficiency of the 1980s; it may even strengthen them.

The Industrial Relations Revolution

These gains centre around the labour market. The 1980s seem to have been the decade when we finally sorted out our industrial relations. Strikes, as everyone knows, have almost disappeared (see Figure 1). Unions are interested in modern co-operative deals with management, involving single-union, plant-wide representation, with arbitration provisions which often rule out strikes altogether. Workers only join unions that are committed to raising their living standards through such intelligent co-operation; as a result many firms have their own workers' association and many unions have lost members, hence their new attitudes. Even Bevin's Transport and General, once the brawny terror of the Docks, felt compelled to participate (if unsuccessfully) in the 'beauty contest' Toyota held for its new Derbyshire plant. What a symbolic triumph of the new order!

But this is just a triumph of commonsense, since it is self-evident that co-operation yields gains, available to be shared between shareholders, managers and workers. What has surprised many researchers brought up in the soft left tradition of British labour economics is just how large these gains have been in the 1980s.

Professor David Metcalf of the London School of Economics recently completed a study[1] of labour behaviour in 329 British firms

---

[1] P. Gregg, S. Machin and D. Metcalf, *Signals and Cycles: Productivity Growth and Changes in Union Status in British Companies, 1984 to 1989*, Discussion Paper No. 49, Centre for Economic Performance, London: LSE, August 1991.

Figure 1: Industrial Disputes: Days Lost, 1970-91
(Per Thousand Employees in Employment)

from 1984-89. This complemented previous studies by Professor Stephen Nickell of Oxford University and Dr Sushil Wadhwani,[2] also of the LSE, for 1975-86. The key finding of the earlier work was that unionised firms raised productivity sharply (about 2 per cent per annum faster than non-unionised firms) in the early 1980s. The Metcalf study found that they did so further in the late 1980s.

It also found that firms which reduced the status of unions, for example by derecognition or withdrawal of a closed shop, obtained still higher growth. If they were also subjected to enhanced competition, they did better still, though this is a less robust result. The gain from these factors added up to no less than 1·8 per cent a year, 9·2 per cent over the whole five years.

The two studies together suggest that the fastest-improving unionised firms bettered their labour productivity over the whole

---

[2] S. Nickell, S. Wadhwani, and M. Wall, *Productivity Growth in UK Companies, 1975-80*, Discussion Paper No. 26, Centre for Economic Performance, London: LSE, March 1991.

TABLE 1

CHANGES IN LABOUR FORCE COMPOSITION, 1979 TO 1989

	1979 %	1989 %
Proportion of:		
Employees in non-manufacturing	68·6	77·6
Employees and self-employed in non-manufacturing	70·4	79·2
Employees in part-time employment	19·7*	23·9
Employees and self-employed who are non-manual	49·0	55·0
Employees who are women	41·7	48·4

*1978.

Source: K. Mayhew, 'The Assessment', *Oxford Review of Economic Policy*, Vol. 7, No. 1, Spring 1991, Labour Markets.

decade of the 1980s by a staggering 20 per cent, while the average unionised firm improved its performance by no less than 16 per cent.

Causes of the Revolution

This work explains the exceptionally rapid growth of productivity in the 1980s (about 4 per cent per annum in manufacturing until the recession) as the unionised sector returned towards better practice. While we cannot pin down the causes of this return narrowly, we can attribute it to some combination of the new union laws, changing labour force composition, the attitudinal shock of the 1980-81 recession, and the refusal of Mrs Thatcher's governments to subsidise failing firms; the Metcalf study rules out unemployment *per se* as a cause, since the main burst of productivity growth in the second period came in 1988-89 when unemployment fell sharply.

Table 1 shows the main changes in labour force composition over the 1980s.

The rise of non-manufacturing, part-time work, non-manual activity, female participation, and self-employment, all traditionally less unionised areas, has assisted the decline in union power. These trends

Figure 2: Ratio of Non-Manual to Manual Wages, 1976-90
(1979 = 100)

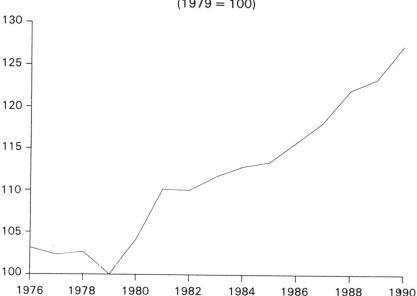

are also reflected in the continued steady rise of non-manual relative to manual earnings (see Figure 2).

As far as the rest of the picture is concerned, there is a mass of anecdotal evidence that management has recovered the 'right to manage', the mirror-image of workers' desire for co-operation. One does not need to refer only to the dramatic changes in the newspaper or the television industries, or in the docks after the brave if long-postponed decision to abolish the iniquitous Dock Labour Scheme. The changes run across the great mass of large firms outside the service sector where previously union practices were the most outmoded. John Purcell of Templeton College, Oxford, details this evidence in the Spring 1991 *Oxford Review of Economic Policy*.[3]

Management thinking shifted in the 1980s towards the ideas of decentralised profit centres responsible for all aspects of their activities, including industrial relations. Small firms and service sector firms

---

[3] 'The Rediscovery of the Management Prerogative: The Management of Labour Relations in the 1980s', *Oxford Review of Economic Policy*, Vol. 7, No. 1, Oxford University Press, pp. 33-43.

TABLE 2

AVERAGE NUMBER OF ESTABLISHMENTS OR
BUSINESSES OWNED BY LARGE ENTERPRISES
IN UK MANUFACTURING, 1958-87*

| | Enterprise size (number of employees) | | | |
	2,000+	5,000+	10,000+	20,000+
1958	12	21	30	44
1978	18	29	42	56
1987	19	31	43	68

Note: *The term 'business' is now used by the Census of Production in preference to
'establishment', recognising the multi-business nature of large enterprises.

Source: 1958: *Historical Record of the Census of Production 1907-1970*, London: HMSO,
1978, Table 10. 1978, 1987: *Census of Production PA 1002*, London: HMSO,
1991, Table 12.

(other than the public sector, of course) had always espoused these
ideas. The change was elsewhere and it was hastened by a wave of
mergers which aggregated often disparate firms into conglomerates like
Hanson or Pearson dominated by the new philosophy. Fortunately, the
UK environment was particularly propitious, indeed may have been
largely responsible, for the new thinking. Table 2 shows that the total
number of large establishments/businesses (over 200 employees)
owned by large enterprises/conglomerates in the UK has increased by
11 per cent since 1978; for very large establishments (over 20,000
employees) the increase was 21 per cent. This, in turn, was after much
larger increases since 1958. But whereas before 1978 these already large
outfits were trying to make a collective national approach work—often
on the basis of strike-containment and other damage limitation—
afterwards they were able to implement the new thinking and were in a
dominant position within the economy when they did so, setting the
tone for nationwide industrial relations (representing an estimated 2·5
million employees).

Rise of Local, Firm-Based Wage Bargaining

As a result, national multi-employer agreements are now a rarity,
whether on their own or mixed with local negotiations. The majority of
wage and other working conditions are negotiated locally, as
demonstrated by Table 3.

TABLE 3

THE FRAGMENTATION OF BARGAINING
ON SELECTED INDIVIDUAL ITEMS OF
PAY AND CONDITIONS, 1979-86

		Single employer only %	Multi- employer only %	Multi- level %
Basic pay	1979	53	12	35
	1986	87	4	9
Overtime	1979	48	32	20
	1986	73	18	9
Shift pay	1979	51	27	22
	1986	76	13	11
Sick pay	1979	81	8	11
	1986	95	1	3
Hours of work	1979	47	35	19
	1986	64	25	11
Holidays	1979	48	35	18
	1986	67	20	13

Source: CBI, *The Structure and Processes of Pay Determination in the Private Sector 1979-1986*, London: CBI, 1988, Tables 8 and 48.

This decentralised firm-based bargaining is commonly referred to as that of 'internal labour markets', where the firm's internal market replaces the outside pressures of a competitive labour market, rewarding employees and attempting to bind them to the firm by firm-specific rewards and training. However, as Stanley Siebert and John Addison note in an accompanying piece in the same issue of the *Oxford Review*,[4] whether these 'internal' markets function well or not depends on how exposed they are to outside competition: if bureaucratic directives (such as the Social Charter) or union laws—or tariffs, VERs, or subsidies— protect certain practices, then that will be reflected by the internal markets. There is nothing *ipso facto* wrong with organising labour within firms; on the contrary, it seems to be a natural way of reducing the 'transactions costs' of doing business with a lot of employees.

---

[4] 'Internal Labour Markets: Causes and Consequences', *Oxford Review of Economic Policy*, Vol. 7, No. 1, Spring, pp. 76-92.

Figure 3: Unionisation Rate, 1955-90

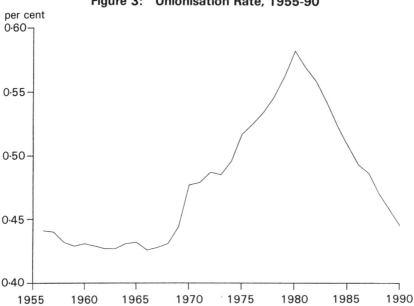

The Effects on the Macro-Economic Scene

What does the improving productivity picture shown by these studies imply for output, employment and unemployment? At Liverpool, we too have found that one of the most powerful explanations of changing worker behaviour is the falling rate of union membership among the employed (union density). This decline, which shows up strongly in our wage equation, is proxying the same weakening of old-fashioned union power and the rise of the new labour co-operation. In 1980 union density peaked at 58 per cent, now it is down to 45 per cent (see Figure 3). For Great Britain alone the rate today is 42 per cent; that is on the Certification Officer's figures. According to the Labour Force Survey it is only 39 per cent. Given that public sector unionisation is about 1·6 times the private sector's, this implies that the private sector union density is only about 28 per cent.

According to our calculations, the combination of this fall in union density with falling marginal tax rates and stable benefits has reduced the attainable ('equilibrium' or 'natural') unemployment rate to about 1 million, against the 2·5 million currently produced by the severe recession. Figure 4 shows the actual and the equilibrium rates for the

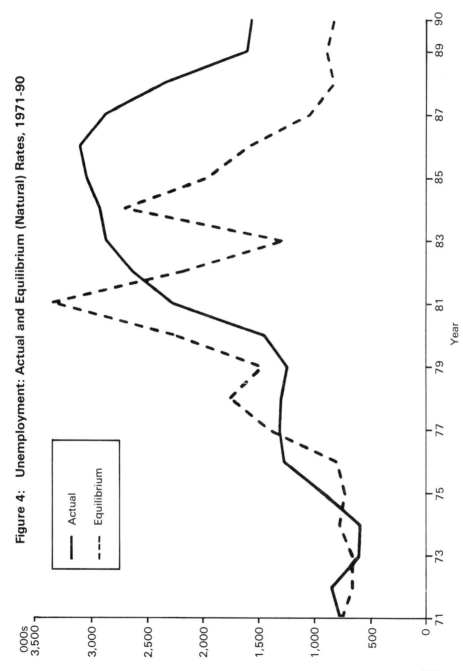

Figure 4: Unemployment: Actual and Equilibrium (Natural) Rates, 1971-90

last two decades. It can be seen that even after the 1980-81 recession the gap between the equilibrium and actual rate only reached 1·2 million. Today it is 1·5 million and rising, with the likely prospect of reaching 2 million by year-end as actual unemployment reaches 3 million.

'Natural Rate' of Unemployment and Inflation

Some economists (notably Professor Richard Layard of the LSE) have tried to calculate the natural rate of unemployment from the behaviour of inflation, using the argument that the Phillips curve relationship between inflation and unemployment is vertical in the long run at the natural rate—in other words, if unemployment were held indefinitely below the natural rate, this would cause ever-rising inflation. So it has been argued that rising inflation is a sign of being below the natural rate, and *vice versa*. This is illustrated in Figure 5.

One difficulty with this method of calculation is that inflation can rise for reasons other than unemployment, namely ('rational') expectations based on the behaviour of policy. If people observe that the government is increasing the money supply rapidly or running large budget deficits which will lead to that result, they will not wait for unemployment to fall before they raise their wage claims and price settings.

Another difficulty is that the influence of unemployment below the natural rate is itself subject to lags. It is powerful when it first occurs and is still a surprise; once it becomes familiar, its effect is incorporated into inflation expectations, where it may well even be perverse because low activity reduces the demand for money and therefore makes a given money supply growth have more impact on prices. What high unemployment, above the natural rate, does imply is steady downward pressure on real wage growth—which we are certainly seeing today, with the latest settlements (November 1991) having fallen to around 5·5 per cent.

For example, rising earnings increases in 1988 and 1989 were largely associated with rising expectations of inflation based on the stimulative monetary policy of 1987-88. Considering the stimulus, one could argue that they were quite moderate, indicating perhaps that the influence of unexpectedly lower unemployment was, on balance, a moderating one on real wages: unemployment was falling until mid-1989 but was on our view above the natural rate.

More recently, there has been a puncturing of inflation expectations,

Figure 5: Unemployment and Inflation

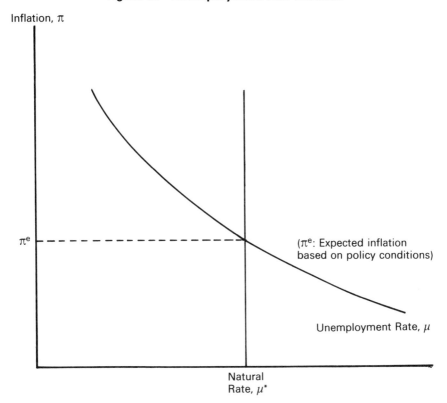

based on the sharp slowdown in money supply growth with its accompanying effects on the housing market. No doubt there has been an additional effect of rising unemployment and the exceptionally large gap between the actual and the natural rate; but the principal impact of this has been in slowing down the rise in real wages.

Conclusion

What all this implies is that the relation between unemployment and inflation is much more tenuous than this method suggests. To get at the natural rate one must estimate the forces of supply and demand for labour themselves and not attempt a short cut through inflation.

What our previous analysis suggests is that declining union power has meant lower wage demands for a given work rate or degree of

Figure 6: Labour Market

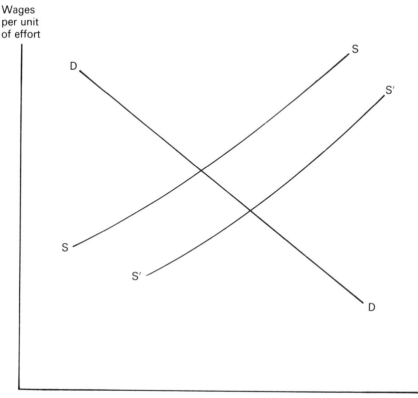

co-operation in higher productivity. In other words, the supply curve of labour has shifted to the right (see Figure 6).

By implication, when one works through the rest of the model, employment and output could be a good 5 per cent higher today without any strains of excess demand, quite contrary to the—at least until recently—fashionable view that inflation pressures are still strong and threatening.

Only the masochism of thoroughly misguided demand management is keeping us from realising this improvement in our capacity to supply.

8

THE CORPORATE SECTOR, THE BANKS AND THE UK ECONOMY

David F. Lomax

Group Economic Adviser,
National Westminster Bank

Introduction

THERE IS A GREAT DEAL of overblown rhetoric as to where the United Kingdom economy should be in Europe. Politicians talk of leading Europe; pessimists talk of our being in the second division. It would suit me if the UK achieved the status of an economic level which was comparable with that of the best in Western Europe. In political terms the UK should be a country which is respected in Western Europe and around the world, and able to exercise the appropriate influence through European and world-wide institutions in the spheres of economics, finance, politics and defence. I have no great desire for us to be wealthier or more powerful than comparable countries in the world such as France, Germany, Italy or Spain. On the other hand, I should be most annoyed if we fell behind those countries or if we were pushed around by them. This ambition, of being in the proper rank of a country of our population, among the OECD countries, is thus positive and realistic. It is not cynical or negative. To achieve that position requires cohesive action towards stated objectives.

If the UK has failings and inadequacies in its present state in comparison with how it would like to regard itself, then this must be

107

almost entirely the result of decisions taken in the post-war period. There is an irrational streak in British thinking which says that the UK has been declining since the mid-19th century, and implies that this process is bound to continue. That analysis of determining the UK situation in the world is entirely divorced from any actions or decisions taken by those more recently responsible for our affairs, whether in government, industry, commerce or finance. Such a point of view seems indefensible in logical terms. Most decisions have their good or ill effects within a four- to five-year period. If we are not satisfied with our current situation, then it seems impossible to conclude anything else but that it is the consequence of decisions we have ourselves taken since the Second World War. Some past measures can be seen as clear follies, such as the 20 years devoted to pursuing the idea of incomes policies.

The Immediate Outlook

In the short term, the UK is facing a slow recovery. The reasons for this are not at all hard to see, and the situation is entirely logical. During the late 1980s the corporate sector was extremely confident. It was increasing sharply its expenditure on investment and on working capital, and was a net taker of money from the financial system, borrowing net no less than £33 billion in 1989. When the then Chancellor pursued the policy of very low interest rates and of shadowing the Deutschemark in the late 1980s, this easing of policy led to a steady expansion of the economy—indeed, real demand grew by almost 8 per cent in 1988—and in turn to a buoyancy of asset prices which led in particular to a house price boom, with the ratio of house prices to income rising to record levels.

When the inflationary consequences of this situation became unacceptable, the Chancellor was forced to slam on the brakes. Precisely because the corporate sector had been absorbing cash net from the banking system and was expanding, so the shock of facing tight money was even more acute. Companies became short of cash. The recession was driven by the need for the corporate sector to save cash. One company may try to save cash by not paying another company. Demand goes down, but the cash shortage remains in the corporate sector until that sector as a whole has saved cash against the rest of the community, such as through lower taxes, lower dividends, lower costs, or increasing profits. Such a recession, generated by a desperate search for cash by the corporate sector, is particularly virulent and particularly hard to forecast in detail. By the second half of

1991 the corporate sector was repaying cash to the banks, thus indicating that on average its cash was under control, but at the same time not implying any great willingness to spend money. This was a key point in stabilising the situation, and in arresting the downturn, but did not indicate necessarily any immediate recovery.

Excess Capacity

The situation has been made worse by the glut of commercial property, a structural situation which might well take three or more years to sort itself out. Likewise, there is excess capacity in retailing and in financial services. The construction industry will obviously face a very lean period, linked to the glut in commercial property.

As far as debt is concerned, the personal sector has a record level of debt. The corporate sector has financial ratios which are now historically at poor levels. The ratio of house prices to income has not yet moved back to the traditional level of 3-3½ times. The savings ratio has recovered, and was averaging 10·5 per cent in the first half of 1991. The housing market is flat, with house prices falling during 1991 and forecast to remain relatively flat during 1992. There is nothing in this situation which would lead one to expect any significant recovery of consumer spending.

The evidence appears to be that the pound is competitive as regards the European currencies at its current exchange rate. The dollar is very competitive, but that is not something which can be controlled by the UK. The same problem is faced by all other European countries. The main problem facing British exports is that world-wide demand is slowing down, in the United States, in Japan, and in Western Europe.

The Role of the Banks

The performance of the private sector has to take place within the objective risk created by the macro-economic environment. If a country generates inflation of nearly 12 per cent one year, followed by a 2 per cent fall in GDP the next year, that is a volatility, an objective risk, which is unusual by OECD standards and substantially increases the risks faced by the private sector. In the UK, heavy extra costs have been borne in corporate failures, redundancies, insurance losses, notably on mortgage protection policies, and in provisions taken by the banks. A significant restructuring of some business sectors could well ensue as a result.

The Basle Ratios

The costs borne by the private sector have raised the question whether the banking system is capable of financing the recovery. Will there be a 'credit crunch'? It may be helpful to look at this situation in more detail. The lending capacity of the banks has to be linked first to the Basle ratios. These capital ratios were agreed initially through the Group of Banking Supervisors meeting at the Bank for International Settlements (BIS) (at one time known as the Cooke Committee), and later agreed through the G10 countries and incorporated into European Community law. These ratios set a rigid relationship between the capital of a bank and its weighted risk assets (WRAs). Summarising, bank capital is divided into two elements, Tier 1 which is essentially equity, and Tier 2 which consists of subordinated debt and other such forms of capital. To calculate a bank's weighted risk assets, its assets are recalculated according to their riskiness. For example, a commercial loan retains its 100 per cent weighting, whereas cash with the Bank of England has a nil weighting. Some off-balance-sheet business is also weighted, so it is possible for the weighted risk assets of a bank to be bigger than its balance sheet. But in general the WRAs of a bank are significantly less than its balance-sheet footings.

So we thus have the situation whereby the weighted risk assets of a bank have a mechanical link with its capital. The authorities specify guidelines for the capital ratios maintained by banks, and the limit below which banks should not go is 8 per cent for Tier 1 and Tier 2 combined. This has led to banks controlling their balance sheets in far greater detail than ever in the past. Controlling the balance sheet, maximising the profit per unit of capital, and allocating business in the most profitable areas, are phenomena which the banks have adapted to with much greater detail and vigour than at any time in the past. Managing the capital and the balance sheet are of crucial importance to commercial banks.

To this should be added the consideration that for much of the 1980s lending to the large corporate sector was unremunerative. It requires a margin of significantly over 1 per cent to cover the capital, administrative and risk costs involved in any loan which is weighted at 100 per cent. Throughout the 1980s the returns received from large companies and more generally in the wholesale markets were far less than that. By the 1990s the banks were thus faced with the twin problems of obtaining an adequate margin on all their business, and at the same time of controlling their balance sheets. It is quite clear where the pressure would first be felt. Some of the large company business was not remunerative. It is much easier to manage the balance sheet through large lines or the Treasury, than in terms of millions of personal or smaller business accounts. Moreover, the small, medium and large company business based on branches is profitable assuming that the risk is adequately controlled.

Efficient World-Wide Financial Market

The world-wide market for financial services and banking is now extremely efficient. A high proportion of corporate lending in the UK, over one-third in sterling, and nearly 80 per cent in foreign currencies, is from foreign banks in London. The large corporate sector has access to the world-wide banking and securities markets. The financial requirements of the large sector are a charge on the capital of the world-wide banking system, and not simply on that of the UK.

There is, in theory, the possibility that the capital of the world-wide banking system would be inadequate for world-wide demand. This would show itself first in an increase in the pricing on wholesale business, and then ultimately in a massive increase in margins. In the meantime, the large corporate sector would have explored all other sources of credit, including all the world-wide securitised markets, such as commercial paper and bond markets. So far we have seen some increases in margins on wholesale business, but not yet even such as to remunerate capital adequately, and certainly no sign of any fundamental shortage of capital in relation to the requirements of that sector. Of course, over the long term a credit crunch could not exist. If margins rose massively at the point of scarcity, then that would attract further capital into the banking industry. So far all we have seen are some steady increases in the cost of money to the large business sector, and no sign whatever of any of the dislocations that would occur if there were a world-wide credit crunch. What we have is a pricing issue, not a quantity or dislocation issue.

The Medium-Term Outlook

This year the UK is likely to grow at about 1·3 per cent, about 1 per cent lower than the rest of Europe. Over the coming five years UK growth could well be comparable with, but perhaps slightly lower than, elsewhere in Europe. We expect a significant current account deficit over this period. The issue is not whether the UK is having bad growth in one particular year, but whether the UK is still on a policy path which prevents it from being able to jump onto the same bandwagon as the other European countries, let alone catch up with them. I do not mind very much if we have a bad year. I mind very much indeed if we simply cannot cope with the competition and do not grow at the same pace as them.

Looking at this from the usual macro-economic point of view, how will UK demand grow? How will international demand grow for our exports? Will our share of world trade be maintained? What identifiable costs will there be, such as contributions to the European budget? These numbers may then be added up to create a macro-economic forecast which may or may not show faster growth in the UK than elsewhere.

We have done this, and the answer is that we expect growth to be somewhat less in the UK than in Europe over the coming five years, combined with a significant current account deficit.

The outlook is thus not particularly good. I should like to broaden the discussion by covering several issues where there is room for further development of our thinking.

Inflation

The first relates to inflation. There is a long tradition of thinking that inflation is technically neutral. In the UK the corresponding approach to macro-economic policy treats price factors mainly as incentives to produce. It assumes that changes may be made in relative prices through policy (such as devaluation) which in turn may produce real and lasting benefits.

Significantly more thought has been given to this, notably by Walter Eltis at NEDO, and these conclusions need to be given greater attention.[1] Inflation is not neutral. Faster inflation significantly increases the risks and the costs to business and is thus a deterrent to investment and expansion.

As far as companies are concerned the tax system is not indexed, so nominal rather than real profits are taxed. Depreciation is inadequate in real terms.

If companies are long on monetary assets, as are banks, then inflation tends to reduce the real capital of the industry concerned.

High inflation and correspondingly higher nominal interest rates

---

[1] W. Eltis, 'How Inflation Undermines Industrial Success', *National Westminster Bank Quarterly Review*, February 1991.

put greater liquidity pressure on companies and persons. It may be that over the complete cycle of a loan, the real cost of paying back a loan is the same. But the existence of higher nominal interest rates has the effect of foreshortening sharply the real cost of repayment of the loan. This means that if policy should be tightened, then there is much greater liquidity pressure on debtors.

To give an example, if interest rates are 5 per cent, a person may be paying 15 per cent of his/her income as interest when buying a house whose value is three times income. If interest rates are 12 per cent then that person would initially be paying 36 per cent of income in buying a house also of a value of three times income. It is quite clear who is more vulnerable.

The same argument would apply in terms of companies borrowing to buy commercial assets. Moreover, high inflation also means a higher risk of policy tightening. Governments are not neutral as regards high inflation. The existence of high inflation makes it more likely that governments will take steps to reduce it. Thus high inflation situations are more likely to be ones of volatile growth in the real economy, volatile movements of interest rates, and volatile movements of asset prices. What better example than the latter part of the 1980s, when we had 12 per cent inflation one year, followed by a 2 per cent fall in GDP the next. Not only do companies have to suffer such effects, but their knowledge of the existence of such risks means that they will increase the risk premia in taking investment decisions.

Monetary Policy and the Real Economy

It is justifiable to attempt to use monetary variables as a means of controlling the real economy, only if you think that relative prices can be changed in a significant and controllable manner by such means. There is, however, not a shred of evidence to validate that point. The profitability and rate of return on British investments are lower than in countries which have pursued quite different policies, such as Japan and Germany.[2] Since there is no evidence that one can obtain any lasting real benefits by such manipulation, there seems to me a very strong case for aiming for a stable low inflation environment, and letting the real economy adapt to such a financial structure.

In the 1980s the UK tried to achieve financial stability through

---

[2] See Walter Eltis, Introduction to NEDO Conference on 'Capital Markets and Company Success', 21 November 1991.

controlling domestic monetary conditions, and letting the exchange rate find its own level. There is a strong theoretical basis for such a policy if it can be carried out effectively. If one is of a monetarist persuasion, however, it would seem to matter not a great deal whether one used an external anchor as the peg for money creation, or a domestic one. If one took the view that real economies adapted to the monetary framework, then the technique for imposing the anchor would seem to matter not a great deal. The main issue would relate to matters of timing. We see now that, through the ERM, the UK is having to adapt to the timing of the German business cycle rather than to that of our own.

However, there is one point in this debate which should not be ignored. This is that over the past decade the British government system was unable to manage an independent money supply policy in an effective and stable manner. The ability to implement a policy in a stable way is crucial in determining what policies one should pursue. We in the private sector have to take the monetary environment as it is given to us through the macro-economic policy of the day.

It is thus not surprising that the industrial, commercial and financial sectors see significant benefits in pursuing the ERM policy with vigour and determination. As far as the private sector is concerned, it does not matter a great deal whether monetary policy comes from a UK source or from an agreed international source. In purely financial terms, the costs to the private sector of a single currency appear very limited indeed. From the point of view of practical convenience it provides benefits to many in the industrial and commercial sectors.

Future Investment

In comparing the UK with other countries, a key point which emerges is that the UK manufacturing sector is relatively small.[3] Its productivity has increased in recent years in line with other major countries, including Japan. In the latter half of the 1980s, total output grew as fast as in other countries. But all this was from a small base. And the cash amount of investment per head in manufacturing industry was significantly lower than in the other countries.

Investment will take place in the UK because of competitive factors which make the UK a better place to invest in, and perhaps because of

---

[3] See Douglas McWilliams and Andrew Sentance, 'The Banks and UK Industry', NEDO Conference on 'Capital Markets and Company Success', 21 November 1991.

a pre-disposition to invest here by companies already with a base here. The capital at the disposal of British companies is clearly less than that at the disposal of German, American or Japanese companies, because their manufacturing sectors are significantly larger, as indeed are their entire industrial and commercial sectors.

This leads to the point that the bait for making the UK an attractive recipient of investment, both by UK and by foreign companies, has to be the underlying efficiency of the system as a whole. In this regard the record of the UK has not been as good as it should be in many areas, including particularly in relation to education and training, and as regards the transport and communications infrastructure.

The argument heard in public discussion that infrastructure investment should take place only where the private sector can afford it, is validated by no respectable economic theories that I know of, and is indeed a travesty of any kind of market economics. The fact that people can now talk of London, as some do, as being a city not of the highest quality is scandalous and should never have been allowed to happen. The infrastructure debate, for example, regarding linkages between Scotland and London by road and rail is both pathetic and destructive. Achieving the highest quality infrastructure and the proper standard of education and training should be something which all of goodwill should as a matter of course see as the desired objective. Achieving that may well require a change of direction throughout the governmental system.

Conclusion

In conclusion, the UK will continue to grow roughly in line with, but perhaps slightly less fast than, the rest of Europe over the coming years. There will be continuing adaptation of our economy to the Single Market and to the ever closer integration in Western Europe. The UK will need to turn its back on some of its past policies, notably the urge to use financial manipulation as an alternative to serious thinking about policy. There will need to be emphasis on the factors which support the underlying efficiency of the economic system, notably education and training on the one hand, and the infrastructure on the other.

9

THE EMU TREATY: SOME ECONOMIC REFLECTIONS

Geoffrey E. Wood

Professor of Economics,
City University Business School

David B. Coleman

Group Economist,
Union Discount Company of London plc

Introduction

BEFORE THE EMU TREATY was signed at the end of 1991 there was extensive discussion of which countries would sign it. There was also some (albeit rather more limited) discussion of whether European Monetary Union (EMU) was a good idea—either in principle or, if desirable in principle, necessarily desirable in the near future. Understandably, discussion of the form such a treaty would take was both limited and, when it took place at all, in rather general terms. Now that a Treaty has been signed, however, an examination of some of the details is appropriate. Such an examination is the aim of this paper. After a brief review of the present members of the Exchange Rate Mechanism (ERM) and of their economic performance in the recent past, several issues are considered.

The first is the set of 'convergence conditions' for membership of EMU. Are such conditions necessary at all and, if they are, have the correct ones been chosen? Next we turn to the objective of the European Central Bank (ECB). It is supposed to achieve price stability;

how can that be achieved and what exactly does price stability mean in this context? That discussion in turn leads to the relationship of the ECB with government—in particular, to its 'independence' and the division of responsibilities between it and Ecofin (the Council of Finance Ministers). It is useful also at that point to look at the micro-economic aspects of monetary union, and to ask what supervisory and regulatory responsibilities the ECB should have. A natural corollary of that is to consider the structure of the ECB itself: Is a 'federal structure' necessary?

Before concluding, two broad economic issues are examined. Will fiscal transfers be necessary to make the system function? (Here a comparison with the Gold Standard is made.) And how will the tax revenue lost by monetary union be replaced?

The concluding section of the paper draws out the implications of the answers to the above questions.

1. The State of the Economies

The initial participants in the Exchange Rate Mechanism (ERM) in March 1979 were Belgium/Luxembourg, Denmark, France, Germany, Ireland, Italy and the Netherlands. With the exception of Italy, each participating country was committed to hold its currency within a margin of 2·25 per cent on either side of the agreed bilateral central rates against the other participating currencies. The Italian lira was allowed to fluctuate in a wider 6 per cent band but in January 1990 moved to the narrow band. In addition to the original membership, the ERM now includes Spain, which joined the mechanism on 16 June 1989, and the UK, which joined on 8 October 1990; both the peseta and the pound are allowed to fluctuate within the 6 per cent band.

Tables 1-6 (below, pp. 133-135) summarise the macro-economic performance of these economies over the last five years. The tables suggest, and more detailed analysis (for example, Goodhart, 1991) confirms, that the high-inflation countries—Greece, Italy, and Spain—have essentially ceased to converge to the performance of the low-inflation core, France and Germany. The most recent data may seem inconsistent with this assessment but this is an illusion produced by the acceleration of inflation in Germany: an acceleration which, on the basis of the Bundesbank's recent behaviour, is unlikely to persist. (The performance even of France is flattered by that acceleration.) Furthermore, unit labour costs have risen faster in these countries than in the core. There has thus been a deterioration in competitiveness as compared with Germany.

This cannot continue indefinitely. A re-alignment would deal with the problem for a time; but unless the inflation rate were reduced, the problem would recur, another re-alignment would be necessary, and so forth. The consequence, of course, would be that the system of pegged exchange rates became less and less credible. Attacks on currencies would be triggered by progressively smaller inflation differences. The system would eventually collapse. A fixed exchange rate system cannot survive in the face of such inflation differences.

Such an analysis may well have led to the conclusion that there has to be 'convergence'—in terms of inflation rates (and also interest rates and budget deficits)—before monetary union can take place. But a set of pegged (or even fixed) exchange rates is different in some respects from a common currency. Is requiring 'convergence' one of these differences?

2. Convergence Conditions

(i) Are They Necessary?

It is useful to distinguish rather sharply between the monetary and the fiscal conditions. First, we consider the monetary conditions. When a country joins a monetary union, its own currency vanishes: the country ceases to have an inflation rate of its own, and has instead that of the union. This of course means that any pre-union inflation difference is eliminated, regardless of the size of the difference, by the act of union. Comparison with the currency union of East and West Germany illustrates this point as, too, does examination of the monetary reconstructions after the great inflations that took place in Continental Europe in the years between the First and the Second World Wars. But these two comparisons also illustrate other parts of the process of union.

Unemployment has risen in what was East Germany. There are many causes of this, but among them is the fact that money wage bargainers had become habituated to compensating for pre-union inflation (Neumann, 1991). Unit labour costs continued to rise, so causing unemployment. Unless the act of joining the union radically changed labour market behaviour, joining *before* rates of increase of prices and money wages were similar would cause rising unemployment. What evidence there is suggests that joining a fixed exchange rate system has little effect on wage bargaining. Thus convergence seems to be necessary on labour market grounds.

The end of hyperinflations illustrates the other reason for requiring convergence. By the time these inflations were ended, there were no long-term contracts denominated in the inflating currency. Its value was collapsing too fast and too unpredictably. That is (fortunately) not true in Europe today. There are long-term contracts in existence—insurance and government bonds are two examples—which are premised on (*inter alia*) nominal interest rates which include a certain expected inflation premium. Converting to a new currency which would have a radically different inflation rate would produce sharp and large redistributions—from debtors to creditors or *vice versa*, depending on whether the joining country was above or below the Union's inflation rate before it joined. A simple illustration shows how large the redistribution could be. Consider a long-term bond in Britain which yields 9½ per cent. If this includes (as it approximately does) an inflation compensation of about 7 per cent per annum, its price would rise by over 100 per cent if the inflation compensation suddenly fell to, say, 2 per cent per annum.[1]

As will be argued below, an inflation rate of 0-2 per cent per annum is a defensible objective. Hence there is another reason for convergence—to avoid this economically (and probably socially and politically) damaging arbitrary rewriting of contracts.

To summarise on the monetary preconditions, then, it is fair to say that they are sensible—despite rather than because of historical precedent. Were there no nominal wage inertia and no long-term nominal contracts, they would be totally irrelevant—but such contracts are a pervasive feature of the world.

Is Fiscal Convergence Necessary?

What of fiscal convergence? The key question here is whether the debts of any national government can have an adverse effect on the taxpayers in other countries of the Monetary Union. Suppose the ECB has no obligation to monetise debt—it cannot be pressed to issue money in exchange for government debt, either directly or indirectly (the latter by holding interest rates steady in the face of debt sales). Then a government with a large amount of debt would not have access to the 'printing press', could not cause inflation, and thus could not impose that cost on the rest of the Union.

---

[1] At the time of writing, 2½ per cent consols stood at a price of £25·88, and yielded 9·66 per cent. Were the yield to fall to 4·66 per cent, the price would rise to £53·65—a rise of 107·3 per cent.

Are there any other costs? Again the answer is 'no'. If a government borrows substantially, and drives up interest rates, it may attract capital from elsewhere in the Union, thus crowding out investments there. But it does so by offering a higher rate of return than these investments. It can do so by having genuinely attractive investment projects, or by being willing to use its taxpayers' money to make otherwise un-attractive projects attractive to investors. Only in the latter case is there a problem—and even then, it is for their own taxpayers (and presumably voters)—but there is no *external* problem.[2,3]

So far discussion has been of a deficit which is 'large' but sustainable. It is not one which is growing so rapidly that it can eventually be serviced only by money creation. This latter is, perhaps, a somewhat peculiar case to analyse in the present context. After all, if the government has no access to the printing press, it would be unable to sell any debt at all if the financing of it manifestly required such access. But markets do make mistakes. Information is not always complete. Suppose such a deficit does emerge, constrained only by gradually rising interest rates until it is realised just how dire the situation is. There is a collapse in the price of the debt—it becomes worthless. Are there any consequences elsewhere? The answer has to be 'no'. There may be a flight to quality, perhaps even to cash, elsewhere in the Union, but that would be transitory, and even the latter case need cause neither banking nor inflationary problems if the ECB satisfactorily carried out its rôle of lender of last resort.[4]

Accordingly, requirements for fiscal convergence are unnecessary. Indeed, it is worth observing that they may be counterproductive. Suppose a country accepts these rules, and then has a 'temporary'

---

[2] See Wood (1990), for detailed discussion of this point; and Lal (1990), for a stimulating discussion of international externalities more generally.

[3] Another reason for arguing that budget deficits be controlled may be the belief that if one country runs a big deficit, it will pull up interest rates for every country in the Union, thus imposing a cost on them in terms of interest transferred abroad and of investment forgone. This is inconsistent with evidence from the United States. The bonds of different states and municipalities sell on different terms, reflecting credit ratings. Further, a forthcoming study (Cook and Spellman) shows how financial markets in the US distinguish between government paper and paper with a government guarantee which is not quite certain or quite complete, or is possibly costly to enforce.

[4] Although quite separate from regulation and supervision, this rôle is, for reasons made clear there, discussed in the section of this paper which looks at these issues (below, Section 5, page 127).

problem. In the presence of these rules, it could turn to its fellow Union members and ask for 'temporary' assistance—aid to avoid breaking the rules. In the absence of rules on deficits, it would have no such pretext for seeking hand-outs.

Summarising, then, inflation convergence is necessary; fiscal convergence is not.

(ii) Are the Convergence Criteria Appropriate?

This question is relatively straightforward. The inflation convergence (and long-term interest-rate convergence) rules are appropriate. Their justification does, however, lie not in terms of inflation convergence being necessary in itself, but in the existence of long-term (explicit or implicit) contracts. It would have made for greater clarity to have defined the convergence requirement in terms of interest rates and wage behaviour—but inflation is a good proxy for the relevant aspects of these variables.

As for fiscal rules, they are at best unnecessary, and quite possibly damaging: damaging to the Union, and damaging also to countries which may quite rationally wish to borrow in the face of fluctuating tax receipts or even (unlikely as this is in the case of governments) productive investment opportunities.

3. The Objective of the ECB

The ECB is supposed to aim at price stability. This is highly desirable. Volatile inflation, or even steadily rising prices, do nothing beneficial for economic performance. It is sensible to be opposed to them (see Grossman, 1991). But what exactly does it mean to say: 'Aim at stable prices'?

There are three separate issues.

o What level of money stock is appropriate on the formation of the Union?

o What price level behaviour is actually meant by 'stable prices'?

o And how will the price level be measured?

The first question has been discussed elsewhere by one of the present authors (Wood, 1990). Briefly, the problem is that, when a new money replaces the old, it is hard to see how the ECB will know the desired money/income ratio at any interest rate, and thus the level of money stock with which to start. This is, of course, because the new money will *not* be simply a change of unit, but will either be or be thought to be—convergence is important here—a money with new characteristics.[5] Crucial among these new characteristics are expectations of future inflation and inflation instability. Even if it were known how these expectations were affected by the formation of the Union, the result for money demand relations in the member-countries would be known only very imprecisely. The effects on expectations will, of course, be unknown; they cannot be otherwise. Hence it follows that the effects on money demand functions will be unknown; and hence in turn that the ECB will have no idea how much of the new money should be issued in replacement for the old so as to maintain price stability.

Alan Greenspan, Chairman of the Board of the Federal Reserve System, has provided (in recent Congressional Testimony (1991)) a definition of stable prices: that rate of price level change which people are happy to neglect in their calculations. What sort of rate of change is that? In fact, it appears as if there can be quite big year-to-year fluctuations—falls and rises—so long as there is a roughly horizontal trend. This is shown by Britain over the years 1870-1914.

Chart 1 shows how prices varied year by year, but with a steady downward drift followed by a steady upward drift, ending roughly where they started. How do we know this did not affect behaviour? Chart 2 shows the consol yield over the same period (after adjusting for Goschen's conversion). It was very stable, unaffected by the year-to-year fluctuations. In other words, what matters is stability over a period of years.

A simple practical rule would be to aim at a price trend of 0-2 per cent per annum—because what studies there are (they are few) suggest that price indices make inadequate allowance for quality change, and are thus biased upwards by that amount. There is, as Charts 1 and 2 make clear, no need to aim at short-term month-by-month price stability.

Finally on this issue, which price index should behave that way? Here we come to a substantial practical problem. For each country in the EEC currently has its own measures of the price level. Each of these has a different composition—in terms of contents and of the weighting of common commodities. There are also two important

---

[5] Price level stability can in principle be attained by importing it—by pegging to a low inflation country. Whether this is possible in the case of Europe is discussed in the context of ECB/Ecofin relations (below, Section 4, page 126).

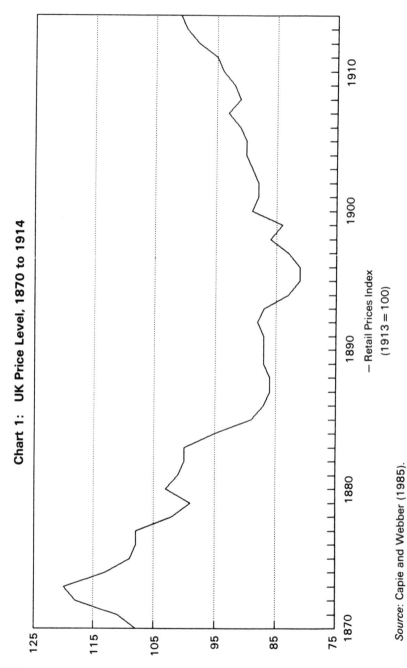

Chart 1: UK Price Level, 1870 to 1914

— Retail Prices Index
(1913 = 100)

Source: Capie and Webber (1985).

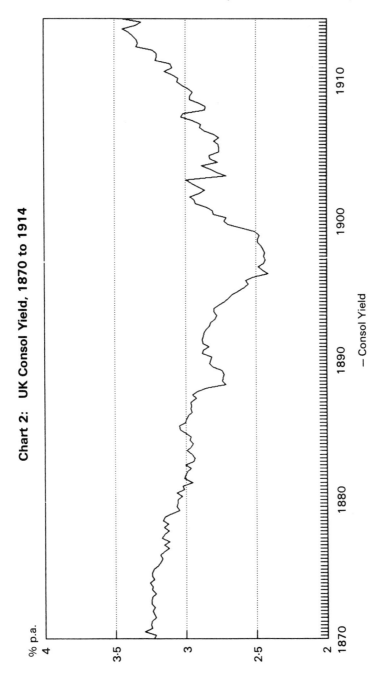

Chart 2: UK Consol Yield, 1870 to 1914

— Consol Yield

Source: Capie and Webber (1985).

conceptual differences. These are with regard to the treatment of seasonal goods, and the treatment of imputed rental from house occupation.[6]

The value of money—the price level—cannot be stabilised in terms of *all* of these indices. Which one will be chosen? Or will a 'European' price index be constructed? Neither solution is altogether satisfactory. If a national index were stabilised, this need not mean price stability elsewhere. And if a European index were constructed it could differ radically from what people were accustomed to. In other words, even if the value of money in terms of some index were stabilised, it could very readily seem a meaningless stability to most people. There is no manifest solution to this dilemma until tastes have converged sufficiently for some common index to prove at least roughly acceptable. It is thus not going to be easy to make the goal of price stability operational for some years to come.

4. ECB and ECOFIN

The ECB is to be 'independent' of governments, as must be the current national central banks before they merge into the ECB. Presumably what is meant by this is a relationship like that between government and the judiciary; laws are passed by government, and implemented by the judiciary without further interference or instruction. The idea underlying this is that politically dominated (or influenced) monetary policy has been inflationary. Models can be constructed to show why this may be so; and there is evidence to support the conclusion, although until the past two decades the evidence was less strong (see Capie and Wood (1991, *op. cit.*), and Capie, Mills and Wood (1992)).

There is, however, a problem over relations with Ecofin. The Treaty gives Ecofin responsibility for exchange rate policy. What exactly that responsibility will comprise is not clear; there are at least two possibilities. There is choice of exchange rate régime, and there is discretion over foreign exchange market intervention.

If the exchange rate régime is other than floating, then monetary policy is constrained by the country to which Europe is pegged. The mandate of the ECB would be meaningless. It would, incidentally, be difficult—probably impossible—for Europe to import price stability in this way; Europe would be too large. The argument is developed at

---

[6] See the OECD's *Consumer Price Indices; Sources and Methods*, and Turvey *et al.* (1989).

length in Neumann (1991, *op. cit.*), but can be summarised as follows. The 'price leader' has to be large relative to its followers so that it can offset by open-market operations in its own money market any inappropriate monetary policy acts by other countries. Hence Germany can be a leader, but Luxembourg, say, could not.

If the exchange rate régime were floating with intervention, then there would be problems. Intervention can be sterilised or unsterilised—that is, its effects on the money stock can be offset by open-market operations, or they can be allowed to persist. Only the latter, unsterilised intervention, has any discernible effects on exchange rates (Schwartz, 1992; Obstfeld, 1990).

So if the exchange rate intervention is to affect the exchange rate, it must affect the money stock. Hence Ecofin must be able to affect monetary policy. But monetary policy is the responsibility of the ECB, which is supposedly independent of the governments of which Ecofin is a part.

There is a contradiction here, and it would have to be an extraordinary set of circumstances, persisting year after year, for the contradiction not to produce conflict. With this division of responsibility between the ECB and Ecofin, the monetary union treaty is unworkable.

5. Supervision, Regulation, and the Lender of Last Resort

The ECB will have responsibility for the stability of the currency within Europe. This will mean that it will have to be ready to act as lender of last resort (LLR). Clarity over what this means in practice is essential, otherwise we are in danger of having an homogenised, over-regulated and inefficient banking system.

The rôle of the lender of last resort is to supply cash to the banking system should there be a run on that system—a run by the public for cash because of fears for the stability of banks. The cash is supplied to the banks by the central bank, in its LLR rôle, when the system *as a whole* is short of cash. It is supplied in exchange for good securities.[7]

---

[7] The process was vividly described by Jeremiah Harman, deputy governor of the Bank of England: 'We lent it,' said Mr Harman, on behalf of the Bank of England, 'by every possible means and in modes we have never adopted before: we took in stock on security, we purchased Exchequer bills, we not only discounted outright, but we made advances on the deposit of bills of exchange to an immense amount, in short by every possible means consistent with the safety of the Bank, and we were not on some occasions over nice. Seeing the dreadful state in which the public were, we rendered every assistance in our power.' (Quoted by Walter Bagehot in his *Lombard Street* (1873), p. 73.)

The total of the money stock stays roughly unchanged, but its composition, as between cash and bank deposits, alters—towards cash if there is a panic, away from cash as the panic abates. This is the rôle as described by Walter Bagehot (1873); discussed by, for example, Rockoff (1986); and carried out by, for example, the US Federal Reserve in 1987.

It should be noted that the rôle does *not* require any monitoring whatsoever of the banking system—only of the quality of securities offered. The Bank accepts responsibility for the supply of money, but *not* for any individual bank. The ECB will be the only source of cash in the monetary system, so it must have that LLR rôle. But to fulfil that rôle it does not require to supervise and regulate banks.

The implication is that supervision and regulation need not be centralised (although the LLR rôle must be). Different regulatory conditions could prevail in different states of the Union—just as they do for state chartered banks in the USA. The benefit of this is that there could be regulatory competition. Different frameworks of different degrees of stringency would be on offer. Banks and customers could choose which they preferred. Banking supervision is not an exact science; there is no known formula for doing it correctly. Hence competition, a discovery process which could help improve regulation, is desirable. (Note that it should not be taken for granted that there should be any supervision at all—other than that operated by bank customers through *caveat emptor*. The evidence for regulation actually achieving anything is rather slight: see Benston (1991), or for a discussion in the European context, Capie and Wood (1991).)

To conclude, then, the ECB *must* act as lender of last resort. But that does not require it to engage in bank supervision and regulation. Whatever supervision and regulation there is should be left to separate, *competing*, not colluding, national authorities.

6. Federal Structure?

The US Federal Reserve has a federal structure. Should the ECB? It probably will, so as to preserve at least the appearance of national central banks. But this is, of course, totally unnecessary in *economic* terms. First, the US structure was established primarily to get round the laws prohibiting interstate banking. The purpose it has now is partly economic and partly political. The regional banks contribute data on their regional economic conditions; this can inform interpretation of aggregate national statistics. But a federal structure, while it can achieve that, is not, of course, essential to achieve it. Secondly, it allows decision-makers from outside the intensely political atmosphere of Washington—a city with no activity but politics—to have a voice and sometimes an influence. Unless there is to be such political centralisation in Europe, there will be no such benefit from the ECB having a federal structure.

Preservation of national central banks within the ECB serves no purpose other than to provide a particulary splendid fig leaf to cover the nakedness of national policy-makers with regard to monetary policy.[8]

7. Fiscal Transfers, the Gold Standard, and Tax Revenue

This paper has so far concentrated on aspects of the Union Treaty itself. In this penultimate section, certain neglected but important implications of that Treaty are noted.

Many commentators write as if EMU were like the Gold Standard, a rule by which price stability would be maintained. As, almost alone, Martin Wolf of the *Financial Times* has pointed out,[9] it is not at all like that. The Gold Standard was adopted (and abandoned) unilaterally, not by international treaty with obligations to fellow signatories. Further, under the Gold Standard, governments had not accepted implicitly or explicitly any obligation on employment levels. Hence the standard was maintained for the sake of the long-term benefits it was thought to bring, generally without regard to employment problems. There were no subsidies to employment, attempts to affect demand by fiscal policy, efforts at incomes policies, and so forth.[10] Nor was there any pressure on Gold Standard countries to make transfers from one to another to alleviate the consequences of sticking to the rule. There were, however, substantial private sector capital flows under the Gold Standard (see Wood and Mudd (1978) for a review). These occurred because a country's likely adherence to the standard could be judged by the state of its government's finances. Unemployment would not provoke devaluation. Hence unemployment was a signal that resources were available which could profitably be combined with capital.

---

[8] Money market assistance can be provided from the centre now that electronic dealing, and, of course, the telephone are in common use.

[9] M. Wolf, 'Federalism before the Fall', *Financial Times*, 3 December 1991, p. 19.

[10] Problems of specific industries were sometimes addressed, but never by 'reflation' or attempts to manage the general level of demand.

In an area with strong commitments to 'social policy', with taxpayers' funds being channelled to prop up declining industries, the likelihood of private capital flows being so substantial is greatly diminished. There will be demands for assistance financed by funds raised from taxpayers.

Transfers of such funds do take place in existing federal systems; and there will surely be pressure for them within Europe as countries from time to time experience high unemployment rates.[11]

There will thus be increased demands on tax revenue—just at a time when one source of that revenue, the inflation tax, is removed from the control of national governments. For some governments this is not a great loss—but for others (notably Greece) it is very large. What will replace it? Will spending be cut?

Surely this will exacerbate pressures for some inflation by the ECB, and give ample ground for quarrels over the distribution of seignorage and, if there is any, the revenue from the inflation tax.[12]

8. Overview and Conclusions

This paper has taken as given that Europe is going to proceed to monetary union, and has considered whether the Union Treaty is well designed to achieve that goal. The overall conclusion has to be that it is not particularly well designed. In particular, the monetary convergence conditions are not well specified, while the fiscal ones are possibly harmful. It is not clear that the objective of price stability for the ECB is readily definable; and how to achieve it is not straightforward, given the monetary disturbances that forming the Union will inevitably entail. The relationship between the ECB and Ecofin is at best disruptive of the orderly conduct of policy. There is a threat of over-regulation of the banking system. And the fiscal consequences of EMU are both serious and largely neglected.

All-in-all, whatever one's view of the objective of EMU, the Treaty which is intended to produce the Union gives cause for concern. It does not seem as well thought out as one would wish of a

---

[11] See Goodhart (1991), *op. cit.*, for a useful elaboration of this point and a survey of the evidence on transfers within the USA and Canada.

[12] The desire for tax revenue is another reason for decentralising supervision and regulation of banks. Even without inflation, seignorage can provide revenue; the desire to increase seignorage gives an incentive to have excessive reserve requirements on banks. Regulatory competition would hold this in check.

Treaty with an objective so disruptive of existing institutional arrangements. Indeed, it could be said that the Treaty bears the hallmark of politically inspired haste rather than of statesman-inspired judgement.

REFERENCES

Bagehot, W. (1873): *Lombard Street: A Description of the Money Market*, H. S. King; reprinted in Norman St. John Stevas (ed.), *The Collected Works of Walter Bagehot* (15 vols.), Vol. 9, pp. 45-233, London: Economist Publications Ltd., 1986.

Benston, G. J. (1991): 'Does Bank Regulation Produce Stability? Lessons from the United States', in F. H. Capie and G. E. Wood (eds.), *Unregulated Banking: Chaos or Order?*, London: Macmillan Press.

Capie, F. H., T. C. Mills, and G. E. Wood (1992): 'Central Bank Independence: An Exploratory Analysis of Historical Data', City University Business School, Department of Banking and Finance, Working Paper, March.

Capie, F. H., and G. E. Wood (1990): 'Financial Structure in a Changing Regulatory Environment: Europe after 1992', in *Game plans for the 1990s*, The 26th Annual Conference on Bank Structure and Competition, Federal Reserve Bank of Chicago.

Capie, F. H., and G. E. Wood (1991): 'Central Bank Dependence and Performance: An Historical Perspective', *Central Banking*, Autumn, pp. 44-63.

Cook, D. O., and L. J. Spellman: 'Repudiation risk and restitution costs: Toward understanding premiums on insured deposits', *Journal of Money, Credit and Banking* (forthcoming).

Goodhart, C. A. E. (1991): 'The Economic Consequences of John Major and Norman Lamont', *Financial Markets Group Special Paper*, No. 90, London School of Economics.

Greenspan, A. (1991): Congressional Testimony.

Grossman, H. I. (1991): 'Monetary Economics: A Review Essay', *Journal of Monetary Economics*, Vol. 28, No. 2, October, pp. 323-45.

Lal, D. (1990): *The Limits of International Co-operation*, 20th Wincott Memorial Lecture, IEA Occasional Paper No. 83, London: Institute of Economic Affairs.

Neumann, M. J. M. (1991): 'Can Germany Anchor Prices in Europe?', *The Global Asset Manager*, London: Credit Suisse Asset Management, Autumn.

Obstfeld, M. (1990): 'The Effectiveness of Foreign Exchange Intervention: Recent Experience 1985 to 1988', in W. H. Branson, J. A. Frenkel, and R. Goldstein (eds.), *International Policy Coordination*, Chicago: University of Chicago Press for the National Bureau of Economic Research.

Rockoff, H. (1986): 'Walter Bagehot and the Theory of Central Banking', in F. H. Capie and G. E. Wood (eds.), *Financial Crises and the World Banking System*, London: Macmillan Press.

Schwartz, A. J. (1992): *Monetarism and Monetary Policy*, IEA Occasional Paper No. 86, London: Institute of Economic Affairs.

Turvey, R., *et al.* (1989): *Consumer Price Indices: ILO Manual*, Geneva: International Labour Office.

Wolf, M. (1991): 'Federalism before the Fall', *Financial Times*, 3 December, p. 19.

Wood, G. E., and D. Mudd (1978): 'The Recent US Trade Deficit—No Cause for Panic', *Reserve Bank of St Louis Monthly Review*, April 1978; reprinted in the *Money Manager*, June 1978, and in the Institute of Chartered Analysts, *Digest*, 1979.

Wood, G. E. (1990): 'One Money for Europe: A Review Essay', *Journal of Monetary Economics*, Vol. 25, pp. 313-22.

TABLE 1

ANNUAL INFLATION RATE: EC COUNTRIES, 1985-91

(*per cent*)

	1985	1986	1987	1988	1989	1990	1991
Germany	2·2	3·1	2·0	1·6	2·6	3·4	4·3
France	5·8	5·3	2·9	3·3	3·6	2·7	3·1
Italy	8·9	7·7	5·9	6·2	6·3	7·5	7·2
UK	5·7	3·6	5·0	6·7	6·9	8·4	6·5
Spain	8·5	11·1	5·9	5·6	6·9	7·3	6·6
Netherlands	1·8	0·5	−0·4	1·7	1·5	2·8	3·6
Belgium	6·1	3·7	2·3	1·7	4·6	3·0	3·1
Portugal	21·7	20·5	11·2	11·6	12·8	15·0	14·6
Denmark	4·3	4·6	4·7	4·5	4·3	2·3	1·9
Greece	17·7	17·4	13·8	15·7	14·0	18·2	20·0
Ireland	5·2	6·3	2·5	3·2	5·1	1·6	2·1
Luxembourg	4·1	0·3	−0·1	1·5	3·4	3·7	3·3

Source: OECD and IMF.

TABLE 2

FISCAL DEFICIT TO GNP RATIO: EC COUNTRIES, 1985-91

(*per cent*)

	1985	1986	1987	1988	1989	1990	1991
Germany	−0·9	−1·3	−1·8	−2·1	+0·2	−1·9	−3·6
France	−2·9	−2·7	−1·9	−1·8	−1·2	−1·6	−1·5
Italy	−12·5	−11·7	−11·0	−10·9	−10·1	−10·6	−9·9
UK	−2·8	−2·4	−1·3	+1·1	+1·3	−0·7	−1·9
Spain	−6·9	−6·0	−3·2	−3·3	−2·7	−4·0	−3·9
Netherlands	−4·8	−6·0	−6·6	−5·2	−5·2	−5·3	−4·4
Belgium	−8·5	−9·1	−7·1	−6·9	−6·7	−5·6	−6·3
Portugal	−10·1	−7·2	−6·8	−5·4	−3·4	−5·8	−5·4
Denmark	−2·0	+3·4	+2·4	+0·5	−0·5	−1·5	−1·7
Greece	−13·8	−12·6	−12·2	−14·4	−18·3	−19·8	−17·3
Ireland	−11·2	−11·2	−9·1	−5·2	−3·5	−3·6	−4·1

Source: OECD and IMF.

TABLE 3

DEBT TO GNP RATIO: EC COUNTRIES, 1985-91
(per cent)

	1985	1986	1987	1988	1989	1990	1991
Germany	42·5	42·7	43·8	44·5	43·6	43·6	46·2
France	31·8	33·9	34·2	35·9	36·0	36·6	37·2
Italy	84·0	88·5	92·9	96·1	98·9	98·6	101·2
UK	59·0	58·1	56·1	51·0	45·7	42·8	43·8
Spain	47·6	48·5	48·7	44·5	45·2	44·5	45·6
Netherlands	69·7	71·7	75·3	77·4	77·6	78·5	76·4
Belgium	119·5	123·7	131·3	132·2	129·9	127·3	129·4
Portugal	69·5	68·4	71·6	74·0	71·5	68·2	64·7
Denmark	74·6	67·2	63·9	64·0	63·3	66·4	67·2
Greece	62·5	65·3	71·5	79·7	85·1	93·7	96·4
Ireland	104·7	115·7	118·5	115·4	104·7	103·0	102·8

Source: OECD and IMF.

TABLE 4

SHORT-TERM INTEREST RATES: EC COUNTRIES, 1985-91
(3 months per cent)

	1985	1986	1987	1988	1989	1990	1991
Germany	5·6	4·8	4·9	3·4	5·4	8·3	9·3
France	10·8	13·3	10·6	8·9	8·6	11·4	10·1
Italy	14·5	17·3	11·5	11·7	11·9	12·9	12·1
UK	10·0	11·9	11·2	8·9	13·2	15·1	14·0
Spain	12·2	11·7	15·8	11·7	15·0	15·2	13·4
Netherlands	5·8	5·8	6·1	4·6	5·8	8·6	9·6
Belgium	10·8	9·8	8·3	6·7	7·6	10·2	10·1
Denmark	n/a	9·0	10·3	9·8	8·0	12·2	10·6
Greece	n/a	17·0	17·3	16·3	16·5	18·5	19·0
Ireland	14·9	12·0	14·0	8·8	8·3	12·1	11·9

Source: OECD and IMF.

TABLE 5

LONG BOND YIELDS: EC COUNTRIES, 1985-91

(*per cent*)

	1985	1986	1987	1988	1989	1990	1991
Germany	6·9	5·9	5·8	6·1	7·0	8·9	8·6
France	10·9	8·4	9·4	9·0	8·8	9·9	9·0
Italy	14·3	11·7	11·3	12·1	12·9	13·4	12·9
UK	10·6	9·8	9·5	9·3	9·6	11·1	9·9
Spain	13·4	11·4	12·8	11·8	13·8	14·7	12·4
Netherlands	7·3	6·4	6·4	6·3	7·2	9·0	8·9
Belgium	10·6	7·9	7·8	7·9	8·7	10·1	9·3
Portugal	25·4	17·9	15·4	14·2	14·9	16·8	17·1
Denmark	11·6	10·5	11·9	10·6	10·2	11·0	10·1
Greece	15·8	17·4	16·6	*	*	*	*
Ireland	18·2	18·2	18·0	17·4	16·0	15·6	16·8
Luxembourg	9·5	8·7	8·0	7·1	7·7	8·5	8·2

Source: OECD and IMF.   * = not available.

TABLE 6

UNEMPLOYMENT RATE: EC COUNTRIES, 1985-91

(*per cent*)

	1985	1986	1987	1988	1989	1990	1991
Germany	7·1	6·3	6·2	6·1	5·5	5·1	4·6
France	10·2	10·3	10·4	9·9	9·4	9·0	9·5
Italy	9·4	10·5	10·2	10·8	10·7	9·8	9·4
UK	11·4	11·4	10·4	8·5	7·0	6·4	8·4
Spain	21·8	21·1	20·4	19·3	17·1	16·1	15·8
Netherlands	10·5	10·2	10·0	9·3	8·7	8·1	7·2
Belgium	11·6	11·6	11·4	10·0	8·5	8·1	8·6
Portugal	8·8	8·2	6·8	5·6	4·8	4·6	4·0
Denmark	4·3	4·6	4·7	4·5	4·3	2·3	1·9
Greece	7·8	7·4	7·4	7·6	7·5	7·5	8·8
Ireland	18·2	18·2	18·0	17·4	16·0	15·6	16·8
Luxembourg	2·0	1·5	2·0	1·8	1·0	1·0	1·0

Source: OECD and IMF.

10

FROM EMS TO EMU

Andrew Britton

Director,
National Institute of Economic and Social Research

Introduction

WHEN I WROTE my history of macro-economic policy in Britain, covering the period from 1974 to 1987, which was published last year,[1] I did not find it necessary to devote a great deal of space to the development of the European Community or of the European Monetary System. Britain was, of course, a member of the EEC throughout this period, and indeed a member of the European Monetary System for most of the time, but macro-economic policy, that is to say, the setting of interest rates and public borrowing, was decided in a domestic or a world context, seldom if ever in an explicitly European context.

All that has now changed. Events have moved with remarkable rapidity since 1987. When the next volume in the National Institute series comes to be written it will probably cover macro-economic policy in Britain from 1987 to about the year 2000. It may well be the last volume in the series. If the provisions of the Maastricht Treaty come into full effect, as intended by most of the signatories, there will

---

[1] A. J. C. Britton, *Macroeconomic Policy in Britain, 1974-1987,* Cambridge University Press, 1991.

137

be no more macro-economic policy-making in Britain to record beyond the end of the present decade.

We have now to contemplate a radical change in the policy régime, so radical that we may need to forget much of the experience of macro-economic policy in this country since the War, and approach the subject afresh from first principles. I shall make a modest start in that direction in this paper. We need to consider both how monetary policy could be conducted by a European central bank on the lines agreed at Maastricht, and also how this will affect the more inflation-prone members of the European Union, notably the United Kingdom. What steps can we, or the French, or the Italians, take to ensure that we are accepted as full members of the monetary union—assuming that is what we want to happen—and to prosper within it? This is, I believe, the right context in which to discuss the recent revival of interest in re-alignment, for sterling or for other European currencies. I will touch on that as well in the course of this paper.

In addressing these fundamental questions we must bear in mind the reasons why opinion in this country has moved in the last few years to favour greater monetary integration within Europe, more or less forcing the Government to sign the Maastricht Treaty despite its profound reservations and the outright opposition of some of its members and closest supporters. This represents, as I have implied, a marked contrast with the views which guided policy in this country both in the 1970s and the 1980s.

Independent UK Macro-Policy a Failure

The fact is that the attempts to conduct an independent macro-economic policy in this country since the end of the Bretton Woods system are now seen as so many failures. This goes for the policies of the 1970s (fiscal expansion, exchange rate depreciation and incomes policy) and also for those of the 1980s (monetary targets or the management of nominal GDP). There is a very cogent argument which says that, in the field of monetary policy, the best that any national government can do for its citizens is to tie its own hands.[2] But if you are dextrous enough to tie your own hands, you may also be dextrous enough to untie them again. The point of an international

---

[2] See, for example, F. Giavazzi and M. Pagano, 'The Advantages of Tying One's Hands, EMS Discipline and Central Bank Credibility', *European Economic Review*, June 1988.

agreement is that it is more difficult to reverse, and a monetary union with a single currency makes it as near impossible as it can be. So the British, and also the French, the Italians and the rest are looking to EMU as the most reliable route to price stability.

The other reason for signing the Treaty is simply that the British cannot afford to be left out of the movement to unite Europe. It makes little difference whether the argument is expressed in economic or in political terms. Geography insists that Britain is part of Europe. Claims to belong to an Anglo-Saxon world, separate from Europe, now sound anachronistic. (Anyway, all the Europeans seem to be able to speak English now, so perhaps the time is ripe for us to become Europeans too.) It is indeed doubtful whether the British economy will prosper as part of a European economic and monetary union unless we are prepared to see our society and institutions adapt on similar lines to those of the other member-states.

Price Stability

The institutional framework for monetary union as agreed in the Treaty has been built mainly to a German model. The European central bank will be independent of government and therefore able to distance itself somewhat from political pressure. I say 'somewhat' because the Bundesbank itself is clearly subject to political pressure and no central bank can ever be altogether detached from the society it serves. The overriding aim of monetary policy, written into the constitution of the bank, will be price stability. It is worth pausing for a moment to consider what that expression actually means.

To an economist price stability means zero inflation, a condition in which price rises and price reductions cancel out when aggregated across all goods and services, and across successive periods of time. The precise definition of zero inflation might be questioned, since different price indices typically diverge over time and since most of them do not take adequate account of improvements in the quality of the goods and services they include. Having selected your index, however (and adjusted it for quality change if necessary), the main point is to ensure that it shows no consistent trend over time. It would not be possible to ensure zero inflation in every year, unless prices were subjected to direct controls, but there should be no technical bar to ensuring an average close to zero for periods of, say, five years or more. For that to happen, the index would have to fall in some years, perhaps by several percentage points. Price stability in this sense would clearly be of great advantage to all those who have to undertake medium- or long-term commitments of fixed money value.

Inflation Low, But Not Zero

Price stability in this sense has not been observed in any European economy since the Second World War. Everywhere, including Germany, we observe persistent inflation, with no firm 'anchor' to the price level. No country has felt the need to induce falls in the price level to compensate for earlier price rises, although some countries have been much more successful than others in preventing accelerations in the rate of inflation. Membership of a fixed exchange rate system, or a monetary union, provides an anchor for prices in individual member-countries. Excessive price rises in one period must be compensated by subsequent price reductions, at least in relative terms. The same is not true of the system or union as a whole. That has no anchor, unless steps are taken to provide one.

The Maastricht Treaty and the protocols attached to it take pains to define, precisely and arithmetically, just what measures of convergence are needed before individual member-states are deemed fit to join a monetary union. It is all the more remarkable, therefore, that the aim of price stability is left altogether undefined. There is no 'anchor' in the constitution. The European central bankers will be able, it seems, to define their own target. They will wish no doubt to secure price stability on a definition that will be of most benefit to the European economy and all those who depend on it. But they will also need to set targets they can be reasonably confident they can achieve, and targets which will command the support of public opinion. It would be surprising, therefore, if they tried to achieve a lower rate of inflation on average in Europe as a whole than has been achieved in Germany in the last decade. If so, we should understand price stability to mean a rate of inflation, measured as the average value of consumer spending, of about 2 or 3 per cent a year.[3]

It has yet to be decided how monetary policy to secure price stability will be conducted by the European central bankers, but clearly any unified central mechanism must involve setting uniform interest rates. Even within the exchange rate mechanism as it now is, with the possibility of currency re-alignments still there and with national

---

[3] The average annual rise in the deflator for private consumption in Germany between 1980 and 1990 was 2·7 per cent: see *OECD Economic Outlook*, December 1991.

monetary authorities setting interest rates unilaterally, the 'play' in the system is only about a percentage point or so. Even now the key decisions, setting the level of interest rates for the system as a whole, are those taken by the Bundesbank. At the end of the process of integration exactly the same interest rates, those set by the European central bankers, will hold in all the money markets of Europe. Indeed, the main instrument by which price stability will be secured will be the setting of these interest rates, which will have a pervasive effect on domestic demand in Europe as well as influencing the value of European currencies (or the ECU) against the currencies of the rest of the world. It is, as we know only too well, a hit-and-miss business trying to control inflation by the appropriate setting of interest rates, but it is unlikely that the central bankers of Europe will have any more reliable methods available to them.

'A More Bumpy Ride' in EMU

In each country the monetary authorities have a range of monetary aggregates which they use, to a greater or lesser extent, as a guide to setting interest rates. Within a monetary union it will be necessary to define monetary aggregates for Europe as a whole, since the banking systems of the member-states will become so closely interwoven with one another that national monetary aggregates will become obsolete. But the process of integration may well itself change the velocity of circulation of money, however defined, so that the growth of monetary aggregates will be a misleading indicator of inflationary pressure (as it certainly was in this country in the early 1980s). We should not underestimate the technical problems which the new central banking system will face. They may well achieve low inflation, if they really do give that aim priority. But the result may be greater instability of output growth, a more bumpy ride than the European economies have experienced in the 1980s.

Even in a monetary union the rate of inflation will not be identical in each country. Tables A and B show price indices for each of the four largest European economies corrected for changes in their relative exchange rates. Table A shows the relative prices of manufactured goods produced in different countries which may diverge gradually over time to offset differences in the quality or esteem of goods produced in different countries. Table B shows the relative prices of all consumer goods and services whether traded or not. It is quite possible for the prices of non-traded goods and services (for example rents,

TABLE A

RELATIVE PRICES OF MANUFACTURED GOODS, 1966-90

(fourth-quarter levels (1980 = 100))

	Germany	France	Italy	United Kingdom
1966	94	100	108	99
1967	96	96	109	100
1968	98	96	117	91
1969	96	105	112	88
1970	101	102	110	88
1971	103	99	106	93
1972	102	102	106	90
1973	113	107	103	78
1974	110	100	112	78
1975	105	109	106	80
1976	111	109	104	77
1977	114	103	104	80
1978	114	103	99	84
1979	110	102	99	89
1980	100	100	100	100
1981	97	97	99	107
1982	102	94	100	104
1983	105	93	104	98
1984	103	94	107	97
1985	101	97	104	99
1986	106	100	104	90
1987	106	100	104	89
1988	102	98	102	97
1989	100	97	106	97
1990	100	97	111	93

Source: NIESR database.

retailers' margins, private health and education, and so on) to diverge substantially from the trend of internationally traded goods.

Tables A and B both show relative prices in the UK corrected for exchange rate changes on a declining trend through the 1970s. This was sharply reversed about the time that oil production became

TABLE B

RELATIVE PRICES OF CONSUMER GOODS AND SERVICES, 1966-90
(fourth-quarter levels (1980 = 100))

	Germany	France	Italy	United Kingdom
1966	84	103	113	103
1967	83	109	111	100
1968	87	115	114	88
1969	87	113	113	90
1970	97	95	116	94
1971	98	92	114	96
1972	101	95	113	91
1973	113	99	107	81
1974	115	96	106	83
1975	107	105	106	83
1976	114	107	99	80
1977	117	102	100	80
1978	117	102	99	81
1979	112	101	98	88
1980	100	100	100	100
1981	94	98	99	111
1982	97	94	102	108
1983	99	91	111	100
1984	97	91	116	98
1985	94	93	115	99
1986	98	95	121	88
1987	100	95	122	85
1988	97	92	120	93
1989	95	90	125	92
1990	95	91	128	88

Source: NIESR database.

important to the balance of payments, but then probably resumed at a slower pace. This suggests that within a monetary union, and in the absence of major structural changes like the development of the North Sea, inflation in the UK may have to be somewhat below the European average.

The Costs of Achieving Price Stability

The possibility of achieving a low rate of inflation is, of course, very attractive for countries like Britain, Italy or France which have a record of high rates even in the 1980s. This is, after all, one of the main reasons for the formation of a monetary union in Europe. Anxiety remains, however, that the cost of achieving low inflation, even in the context of monetary union, will turn out to be very high. By an unfortunate coincidence the Maastricht Treaty was signed just at the time when expectations of growth were sharply revised downwards. This is indeed no more than a coincidence: the disappointment of expectations is as evident in North America as it is in Europe. But it is a gloomy background against which to count the output cost of achieving the goals which the Treaty has set. In assessing that cost it is natural to look at what has already been achieved in the course of the 1980s in Britain and also in France, Italy and the other European countries which have come a long way towards 'converging' with Germany.[4]

A fixed-rate system or a monetary union linked to a low-inflation country can help a counter-inflation strategy at three levels. It can require policy-makers to adopt tight fiscal and monetary polices—but if that is all it does then the cost will be the same as if each country had pursued its goal alone. It can reduce expectations of inflation by making the commitment of policy-makers more credible—by tying their hands—which should mean that low inflation is actually achieved sooner and at less cost. Finally, it can lead to changes in the institutions which make some countries more prone to inflation, leading to a more lasting solution of the underlying problem.

Tables C and D show inflation rates and unemployment rates in the major countries of Europe since the late 1970s. There has been a substantial fall in inflation over that period in all the countries shown but there has also been a rise in unemployment. In 1991 the rate of unemployment was under 5 per cent in (West) Germany, compared with 8½ to 9 per cent in the UK, 9½ per cent in France and nearly 11 per cent in Italy. In all these countries (unlike the USA or Japan) unemployment is now substantially higher than it was in the late 1970s.

---

[4] The National Institute organised a conference in December 1991 to assess the implications of the Maastricht Treaty for each of the member-states. The papers are published as R. Barrell (ed.), *Economic Convergence and Monetary Union in Europe*, London: Sage Publications, 1992.

TABLE C

INFLATION RATES (PRIVATE CONSUMPTION DEFLATORS), 1979-91

(per cent)

	1979	1980	1981	1982	1983	1984	1985	1986	1987	1988	1989	1990	1991
Germany	4·2	5·8	6·4	5·3	3·3	2·8	2·0	-0·5	0·6	1·4	3·1	2·6	3·4
France	10·7	13·3	13·0	11·6	9·7	7·7	5·7	2·7	3·2	2·7	3·4	2·9	3·0
Italy	14·5	20·5	18·1	16·9	15·2	11·8	9·0	5·8	5·0	5·3	6·2	6·3	6·4
UK	13·6	16·3	11·2	8·7	4·8	5·0	5·4	4·4	4·3	5·0	5·5	6·0	6·2

Source: OECD, *EC Outlook.*

145

TABLE D

UNEMPLOYMENT RATES (NATIONAL DEFINITIONS), 1979-91

(per cent)

	1979	1980	1981	1982	1983	1984	1985	1986	1987	1988	1989	1990	1991
Germany	2·9	2·5	3·4	5·0	6·6	7·1	7·2	6·4	6·2	6·2	5·6	5·1	4·6
France	6·0	6·3	7·5	8·2	8·4	9·8	10·2	10·4	10·5	10·0	9·4	8·9	9·4
Italy	7·8	7·7	8·5	9·2	10·0	10·1	10·2	11·2	12·1	12·2	12·1	11·2	10·9
UK	4·5	6·1	9·1	10·4	11·2	11·4	11·6	11·8	10·4	8·2	6·2	5·9	8·7

Source: OECD, EC Outlook.

In France, Italy and the UK, however, the increase has been much greater than in Germany, in absolute terms and even proportionately.

Convergence of Inflation Rates and the Rise in Unemployment

Evidence from wage equations estimated at the National Institute suggests that the convergence of inflation rates in Europe is substantially explained by this relative increase in unemployment in the countries with a history of relatively high inflation. In addition, however, there is evidence of a favourable shift in the underlying relationships. This is especially true of Italy, where it seems to be associated with institutional change, in particular with the modification, and partial abolition, of wage indexation under the *scala mobile*.

Some structural change influencing the labour market is inevitable and spontaneous following closer integration of markets for capital and for goods. Exposing more firms to international competition reduces the degree of local monopoly rent which an organised labour force can extract. More and more firms will be in a position to say to their employees that the wage costs of, say, German competitors must be matched or the business will have to close down. The threat to shift production to another country may be as potent as the threat of bankruptcy. If these risks are evident at the level of the individual firm, or wage-negotiating unit, then low inflation may be maintained without the 'discipline' of actual unemployment or spare capacity.

Much broader issues are raised by the possibility that national labour market institutions will tend to become more similar as a result of closer trading relations. The official British Government view is that labour market institutions reflect the very different social conditions and histories of different countries, and that they should be allowed to develop each in their own way. This is not the occasion for a discussion of the principle of subsidiarity, still less the merits of the British labour market relative to that of France or Germany. I would simply make the point that the operation of macro-economic policy may become easier if the behaviour of the different national economies becomes more uniform. Suppose, for example, that there were to be another oil price 'shock' similar to those of 1973-74 and 1979. If wage bargaining in some countries leads to higher wages as a consequence of the rise in fuel prices, whilst wages are unchanged in other countries, then the balance of trade and competitiveness within Europe will be disturbed. In the past this could have been corrected by exchange rate re-alignment;

now it will have to be corrected by a relative shift in levels of demand and economic activity. The more homogeneous the economies of Europe become, the less subject they will be to disturbances of this kind.

Re-alignments Within the ERM

It is abundantly clear that a European monetary union will not operate without friction, stress and strain. It is all too easy to design a system which would work well in the absence of unforeseen disturbance, but there is no reason to think the future world environment will be any less turbulent than the past—if anything the opposite is true. There will be times when governments will regret nailing their flags to the mast of price stability, and they will regret giving up the freedom to devalue their currency. The UK, which has been particularly prone to inflation and devaluation in the past, will probably regret this loss of freedom more than most. And this, of course, is the reason for making the commitment. When policies are 'time inconsistent' one enters into a commitment, knowing full well that one will wish to break that commitment in the future, but still knowing that the commitment is worthwhile.

The case for devaluing sterling has been presented from two very different viewpoints in recent weeks, by Wynne Godley and others in an article in *The Observer*,[5] and by Alan Walters and others in a letter to *The Times*.[6] I have heard the case for devaluing the lira and the French franc presented in rather similar terms. I would like to consider briefly, therefore, the rôle which re-alignments play in the EMS as it is now constituted, and in doing so present some arguments suggesting that a re-alignment would not be the right response to the current situation.[7]

The EMS is neither a fixed-rate system nor a floating-rate system but a hybrid. There is a 'let-out' clause allowing occasional re-alignments, without specifying the circumstances in which they are allowed. The system can work properly only if re-alignments are unexpected, so the monetary authorities have a strong incentive to conceal their true intentions. The markets therefore will pay little

---

[5] 'Route Out of Recession', *The Observer*, 5 January 1992.

[6] *The Times*, 7 January 1992.

[7] For a much fuller presentation of these arguments, see A. J. C. Britton, 'Exchange-rate Realignments in the European Monetary System', NIESR Discussion Paper (New Series) No. 1, November 1991.

attention to what the authorities say, much more to what they do. Information can be conveyed to the markets both by the actions of the authorities when exchange rates change and by the inaction of the authorities when exchange rates remain fixed despite an obvious incentive to change them.

Devaluation and Unemployment Threshold

The motivation of the authorities may in fact be very complex, but it may be useful to consider a much simplified example. Suppose that the authorities have decided to hold the exchange rate unless and until the rate of unemployment crosses some threshold. Until that threshold is actually crossed all that the market knows is that the threshold is somewhere above the highest rate experienced so far. When the threshold is actually crossed and the devaluation takes place the market will be (to some degree) surprised. Until that happens, the authorities will have the benefit of a reputation for toughness—a somewhat exaggerated reputation, in fact. The more effective they think this reputation is, the more reluctant they will be to lose it, and hence the higher the threshold level for unemployment they should adopt. They may well choose such a high threshold that devaluation never takes place at all. In choosing the threshold level, the uncertainty of future events is an important consideration. It would not matter too much perhaps that the level of the threshold was revealed if one thought that this level of unemployment would never be seen again. In an uncertain world, however, I would argue that devaluation is a measure to be used only in dire emergencies—and one never knows when one will be in a worse emergency than the present.

At its simplest the argument for devaluation ignores altogether the effect of one such move on the perceived likelihood of another. But this is of the essence of the decision. A small devaluation now would demonstrate the weakness of the commitment to a fixed exchange rate, without necessarily having much effect on competitiveness. The immediate consequence therefore might well be to increase the expectation of further devaluation, requiring interest rates to rise. A really large devaluation, on the other hand, would totally undermine the credibility of counter-inflation policy, and would also be inconsistent with continued membership of the EMS.

The decision has now been taken to move to a monetary union (even though Britain has still to decide whether to join it), and the timetable has been roughly sketched out. This will change the nature of the re-alignment game. 'Finite period' games are quite different in character from 'infinite period' ones. There is a special incentive to re-align one more time at the last moment, because there is no loss of reputation to worry about if there is in any case no possibility of re-alignments after that.[8] It may be for that reason that the convergence criteria agreed at Maastricht include the requirement that the country concerned has not devalued its currency in the two years prior to entering the EMU. The earliest date for setting up the EMU is January 1997; two years prior to that is January 1995. Presentation of a devaluation as a final adjustment need not be taken very seriously until that date approaches. The Italians have in fact devalued the lira 'for the last time' once already, but relative interest rates show that the market has not believed them.

The case for setting up a monetary union rests on the belief that adjustment of imbalances between the member-countries is possible without changing exchange rates. If this belief is false the project is doomed to fail. Adjustment requires that countries (or regions, or industries) which become uncompetitive should reduce real wages or raise productivity so as to maintain or restore full employment. It is clearly in the interests of the firms and the workers in the country (or region, or industry) to do so. Economists, with their commitment to rationality as an explanation of human behaviour, usually predict that good sense will ultimately prevail. That is the basis for optimism in the present case. We are perhaps on safer ground in saying that, in the absence of good sense, devaluation will not solve the problem anyway because workers will insist on restoring their real wages. The economics profession has become much more willing to support schemes for monetary union, as a result of the disappointing experience with devaluation, especially in Britain, since 1967.

Devaluation may be discredited as a solution to the problem of international adjustment, but the anxiety which lies behind the continuing calls for devaluation is understandable enough. The question remains to be answered: What else can be done to ease adjustment other than simply allowing unemployment to rise without limit in the less competitive or more inflation-prone countries or regions of Europe?

---

[8] See also K. Froot and K. Rogoff, 'The EMS, the EMU, and the Transition to a Common Currency', NBER Working Paper No. 3,684, 1991.

Adjustments Within a Monetary Union

Within a nation state the problem of maintaining regional balance is solved in part by fiscal transfers. Central government tax revenue falls in the region which is uncompetitive, and central government expenditure on unemployment benefit rises. These transfers help to narrow the regional dispersion of real incomes and may also reduce the variation of unemployment rates. No such transfers are envisaged within the European EMU. The Maastricht Treaty makes provision for some enlargement of the regional and social funds, but these are intended to assist the development of regions which are not yet fully integrated with the advanced economy of the rest of Europe.[9] They are not designed to iron out cyclical variations in demand or to bail out the industries of countries which fail to reduce inflation and thus price themselves out of the European market. The regional and social funds are thus of only marginal significance to the British economy, and will do nothing at all to ease our path to full membership of an EMU.

The MacDougall Report[10] suggested that the development of a unified macro-economic policy for Europe should be accompanied by the development of a much larger central community budget. This has not happened because the richer member-states are not prepared to countenance the scale of transfers to the poorer member-states which takes place within one country. We are in fact a long way from building a United States of Europe, despite all the talk about cohesion. The European Union to be set up under the Maastricht Treaty remains a union of distinct political and economic units, a single market perhaps, but not a single economy.

If the member-state is the largest unit within which fiscal transfers take place, then it should also be the largest unit within which wages and prices are fixed. If a market mechanism is to correct imbalances between member-states, then it is imperative that relative wages and prices between states be flexible.

As between regions of the UK, and most other states, changes in relative wages and prices play only a minor rôle in adjustment. Many

---

[9] For a discussion of these funds and the broader issue of cohesion in Europe, see I. Begg and D. Mayes, 'A New Strategy for Social and Economic Cohesion after 1992', European Parliament, D-G for Research, Research and Documentation Paper No. 19, Luxembourg: European Parliament, 1991.

[10] Sir D. MacDougall, 'Report of the Study Group on the Role of Public Finance in European Integration', Brussels: EC Commission, 1977.

wages and prices are still set nationally—especially in the public sector. If wages and prices were to be set at a common level for Europe as a whole, the prospects for adjustment would be very poor indeed. On the contrary, it will be more important than ever to vary wages and prices deliberately in different countries to compensate for differences in productivity and non-price competitiveness, now that exchange rates cannot move to compensate for inappropriate settings.

Ceiling for Budget Deficits 'Remarkably Low'

Fiscal policy within a member-state can cushion the effects of the adjustment to external balance provided that the public sector is permitted to go into deficit when the economy is depressed. Under the Maastricht Treaty a budget deficit in excess of 3 per cent of GDP would normally be considered 'excessive'. This is a remarkably low level at which to set the ceiling. Even the expected German federal deficit appears excessive on this criterion, and so does the scale of borrowing expected in the UK next year. However, the Treaty recognises that certain excuses for deficits in excess of 3 per cent must be accepted as valid.

The deficit should be seen in the context of 'the medium-term economic and budgetary position of the Member-State'. So a case could be made out that a deficit is not excessive when it reflects a temporary recession caused by a loss of international competitiveness. The use of fiscal policy to stabilise output is not altogether ruled out, although the Treaty certainly does nothing to encourage it.

In Britain, the official view now seems to be that the discretionary use of fiscal policy is fraught with difficulties, but that the deficit should rise and fall with the economic cycle in response to 'built-in' stabilisers. The problem with discretionary changes in taxation or spending is that they are difficult to make except to an annual timetable, and that they must rely on economic forecasts. Economic forecasting never was easy or successful; it has become more difficult and more prone to error following the structural changes in the economy in the 1980s. The automatic tendency of tax revenue to fall in a recession, and spending on social security benefits to rise, does not rely on foresight. If we wish to increase the stability of output and employment we should be looking for ways of modifying the tax and expenditure systems to enhance their rôle as automatic compensation mechanisms—provided that the resulting fiscal deficits in recessions do not fall foul of the agreed European definition of 'excess'. And European policy members collectively would do well to take a sympathetic view of deficits which arise in this way.

The underlying reason for wanting to ease adjustment is primarily the pain and suffering caused to individuals by personal bankruptcy and by unemployment. All member-states, and especially the UK, would do well to think of ways of addressing these issues directly now that the scope for macro-economic measures to control aggregate demand at a national level has been reduced. Such measures may well involve sacrificing some of the flexibility of the economy in responding to boom conditions so as to limit the consequential damage in the downturn.

We should look again at the prudential limits to lending and borrowing, both by households and by small businesses. Experience in the current recession suggests that banks lent too freely in the last boom for their own good and for the good of their customers. The national monetary authorities retain responsibility for prudential supervision, although clearly the freedom of capital movement means that regulations in different countries cannot differ very greatly. A case could be made out that prudential control in this country has been looser than in the rest of Europe, and should be somewhat tighter in the future.

A similar, and more controversial, issue could be raised about employment regulation. Do we want an economy in which jobs are easily created in the boom, and just as easily destroyed in a slump? This would make the economy more flexible and help the efficient allocation of resources, but it exposes individuals to uninsurable risks.

Alternatively, do we want greater job security even if this means fewer jobs in total? There is a real choice to be made. Individuals can to some extent choose for themselves, by negotiating their own terms of employment, or through their choice of occupation. Nevertheless, some countries in Europe make job security a matter for regulation. This is part of the debate about the European social charter, and the measures following from it. That debate should perhaps be influenced by the message of this paper about macro-economic policy. The need for individual guarantees against cyclical disturbance to employment is greater if the scope for counter-cyclical control of aggregate demand is reduced.

Conclusions

British participation in a European EMU is supported by a coalition of centre-left and centre-right against opposition from both extremes.

This support reflects a weariness with the recurrent failures of domestic monetary policy, especially with devaluation as a recipe for growth, but also with 'technical monetarism'. But anxieties about the international adjustment mechanism within the EMU remain. The main burden of adjustment must now rest with wage and price flexibility and for that we have to rely in the end on the rationality of decision-taking at the level of the individual firm. But national governments should use what margin of manoeuvre they retain to make adjustment less costly to the economy as a whole, and to the individuals most at risk. This will entail policies to raise productivity, for example, through better training and education, which have not been discussed here. It may also involve some use of fiscal policy, preferably by increasing the stability built into the system rather than relying on discretionary measures. I have suggested that the regulation of credit and of employment contracts may also need reconsideration but, of course, both of these also involve issues of micro-economic policy which are also not discussed here.

The main motive for forming EMU is the desire to unite Europe, politically as well as economically. For that reason we can expect to see far more convergence of institutions and procedures than is strictly necessary for the pursuit of common aims. Even in the field of social policy, where a good case for subsidiarity can be made, the forces making for assimilation are very strong.

The success of EMU depends mainly on the continuing strength of this wish to unite. There will clearly be many difficulties to overcome in the transition from EMS to EMU so the enterprise could be called off unless the participants remain determined to ensure it succeeds. But the alternative to making that transition is not to leave things as they are. If the EMS does not evolve into EMU, then it is unlikely to prove viable for long in its present form.

THE AUTHORS

Mark Boléat was born in Jersey, Channel Islands, in January 1949. He was educated at Victoria College, Jersey, the Lanchester Polytechnic (First-Class Honours in Economics) and the University of Reading (MA in Contemporary European Studies). He is also a Fellow of the Chartered Building Societies Institute. After teaching at Dulwich College and working as an economist for the Industrial Policy Group, he joined The Building Societies Association as Assistant Secretary (Public Relations) in January 1974 and subsequently held a number of positions before being appointed Secretary-General in September 1986. He was appointed to the new position of Director-General in June 1987. He has also been Director-General of the Council of Mortgage Lenders since its establishment in 1989. Mr Boléat was Secretary-General of the International Union of Housing Finance Institutions (formerly IUBSSA), 1986-89, and Managing Director of the European Federation of Building Societies, 1986-88.

He was founder Editor of *Housing Finance International.* His publications include *The Building Society Industry* (second edition, 1986); *National Housing Finance Systems: A Contemporary Study* (1984); (with Adrian Coles) *The Mortgage Market* (1987); *Building Societies: The Regulatory Framework* (1987); *New Lenders and the Secondary Mortgage Market* (1988); and *Housing in Britain* (second edition, 1989). For the IEA he contributed 'The Housing Market' to *The State of the Economy 1991* (IEA Readings No. 34, 1991).

Outside the BSA, he is involved in the voluntary housing movement as a member of the Committee of Management of Tenant Housing Trust since 1977 and its Chairman for three years to October 1988; a member of the Committee of Management of Circle 33 Housing Trust since 1977 and Chairman since September 1990; Chairman of Hillingdon Housing Association since September 1991. He was appointed to the Board of the Housing Corporation in September 1988.

Andrew Britton has been the Director of the National Institute of Economic and Social Research since 1982. Educated at Royal

Grammar School, Newcastle upon Tyne, and Oriel College, Oxford (BA); London School of Economics (MSc). Joined HM Treasury as Cadet Economist, 1966; Economic Assistant, 1968; Economic Adviser, 1970; Senior Economic Adviser, DHSS, 1973; HM Treasury, 1975; London Business School, 1978-79; Under Secretary at HM Treasury, 1980-82.

Mr Britton's publications include: (ed.) *Employment, Output and Inflation* (1983); *The Trade Cycle in Britain* (1986); (ed.) *Policymaking with Macroeconomic Models* (1989); and *Macroeconomic Policy in Britain, 1974-1987* (1991).

Dr David A. Coleman has been Lecturer in Demography at the University of Oxford and a Fellow of Linacre College since 1980. He was at University College, London, 1970-80. He was the Special Adviser to the Minister of Housing and the Minister for the Environment, 1985-87, and Special Adviser to the Home Secretary, 1985.

He has undertaken consultancies on demographic, housing and other subjects for the United Nations, the Home Office and business. He is a frequent writer and broadcaster on housing matters.

He is the author or editor of over 50 papers and four books, including *The State of Population Theory: Forward from Malthus* (ed. with R. S. Schofield, 1988); *Housing Policy: Unfinished Business* (1988); (with J. Salt) *The British Population: patterns, trends and processes* (1992).

David B. Coleman was educated at Luton Sixth Form College and the City University Business School where he gained a First-Class Honours Degree in Banking and International Finance. In October 1988 he joined The Union Discount Company of London, plc, as Assistant Group Economist and in September 1991 became Group Economist. He will shortly be joining the Treasury Advisory Group of the Canadian Imperial Bank of Commerce (CIBC) in London. He was co-author with Nicholas Parsons of 'Government and the PSBR', *Economic Affairs* (Vol. 11, No. 4, June 1991).

Walter Eltis is Director General, National Economic Development Office (NEDO). He was Economics Director (NEDO), from 1986-88, Fellow and Economics Tutor, Exeter College, Oxford, 1963-88.

He is the author of *Classical Theory of Economic Growth* (1984);

Growth and Distribution (1973); co-author with Robert Bacon of *Britain's Economic Problem: Too Few Producers* (1976); and he has published articles on Adam Smith and François Quesnay. For the IEA he has contributed (with Robert Bacon) 'How Growth in Public Expenditure has Contributed to Britain's Difficulties', in *The Dilemmas of Government Expenditure* (IEA Readings No. 15, 1976); 'Public Policy', in *Job Creation—or Destruction?* (IEA Readings No. 20, 1979); 'The Need to Cut Public Expenditure and Taxation', in *Is Monetarism Enough?* (IEA Readings No. 24, 1980); 'British Industrial Policy for the 1990s', in *The State of the Economy* (IEA Readings No. 31, 1990); and 'United Kingdom Investment and Finance', in *The State of the Economy 1991* (IEA Readings No. 34, 1991).

Alan Evans was born in Surrey in 1938. He was educated at Charterhouse and took articles qualifying as a Chartered Accountant in 1960, winning one of the seven certificates of merit awarded in the English Institute's Final Examination. In 1961 he went to University College, London, to read Philosophy and Economics, and, instead of going back to accountancy, went to the University of Michigan for one year in 1964 before returning to University College, London, to research for a PhD in the economics of residential location.

Between 1967 and 1971 he was a Lecturer in the Department of Social and Economic Research at the University of Glasgow, researching in the economics of land-use planning and of city size. From 1971 to 1976 he carried out research at the Centre for Environmental Studies before spending a year at the London School of Economics as an Economics Lecturer.

He was appointed Reader in Environmental Economics at the University of Reading in 1977 and Professor in 1981. He was Dean of the Faculty of Urban and Regional Studies, 1984-87. He is currently Pro-Vice-Chancellor of Reading University.

He is the author of *The Economics of Residential Location* (1973); *Urban Economics* (1985); co-editor of *Public Economics and the Quality of Life* (1977); and *The Inner City: Employment and Industry* (1980). For the IEA he has previously written *No Room! No Room!* (IEA Occasional Paper No. 79, 1988).

Douglas Fraser: After graduating from the Manchester Business School, Douglas Fraser spent 12 years with EMI Ltd. where he held a number of management positions before joining the National Economic

Development Office in 1979, where he has been responsible for work in information technology and engineering before being appointed Industrial Director in 1988.

John Ip joined the National Economic Development Office in 1989. He worked previously for Data Resources, Inc. as an Economic Consultant on both sides of the Atlantic, and for the Economist Group where he managed their Asia-Pacific Forecasting Service in Hong Kong. He is responsible for the economic input to the Office's work with the various Sector Groups and Working Parties, and was appointed Head of Industrial Economics in 1990.

Giles Keating is Chief Economist and a Director, Research, of Credit Suisse First Boston. He holds a BA in Philosophy, Politics and Economics from St Catherine's College, Oxford, and an MSc in Mathematical Economics and Econometrics from the London School of Economics.

He has published a number of articles on macro-economic issues in academic journals, most recently 'A Two-Good Model with Capital Accumulation and a Real Balance Effect', *Oxford Economic Papers* (1987), and 'Capital Asset Pricing under Alternative Policy Régimes', *Economic Modelling* (1988). He writes a regular column for *Nihon Keizai Shimbun* and for *The Times*. He is author of *The Production and Use of Economic Forecasts* (1985). For the IEA he contributed a paper, 'What Went Wrong with UK Demand and Trade Performance? How to Put It Right', to *The State of the Economy* (IEA Readings No. 31, 1990).

Dr David Lomax is Group Economic Adviser, National Westminster Bank, and Editor of the *National Westminster Bank Quarterly Review*. He was educated at the University of Cambridge and Stanford University, California. He is the author (with P. T. Gutmann) of *The Euromarkets and International Financial Policies* (1981); *The Developing Country Debt Crisis* (1986); and *London Markets After the Financial Services Act* (1987). He is the author of numerous articles and a regular broadcaster. For the IEA he contributed a paper, 'The British Economy and Current Weaknesses', to *The State of the Economy* (IEA Readings No. 31, 1990).

Patrick Minford has been Edward Gonner Professor of Applied Economics, University of Liverpool, since 1976. Formerly Visiting

Hallsworth Research Fellow, University of Manchester, 1974-75. Sometime Consultant to the Ministry of Overseas Development, Ministry of Finance (Malawi), Courtaulds, Treasury, British Embassy (Washington). Editor of *National Institute Economic Review*, 1975-76. He is the author of *Substitution Effects, Speculation and Exchange Rate Stability* (1978), and of essays published in *Inflation in Open Economies* (1976); *The Effects of Exchange Adjustments* (1977); *On How to Cope with Britain's Trade Position* (1977); *Contemporary Economic Analysis* (1978); co-author of *Unemployment: Cause and Cure* (1983, 2nd edn. 1985).

Professor Minford is a member of the IEA's Advisory Council. He has contributed papers to *The Taming of Government* (IEA Readings No. 21, 1979); *Is Monetarism Enough?* (IEA Readings No. 24, 1980); *Could Do Better* (IEA Occasional Paper No. 62, 1982); *The Unfinished Agenda* (1986); and *Reaganomics and After* (IEA Readings No. 28, 1989). He was joint author (with Michael Peel and Paul Ashton) of *The Housing Morass* (Hobart Paperback No. 25, 1987), and edited and introduced *Monetarism and Macro-economics* (IEA Readings No. 26, 1987). Most recently he contributed 'The Labour Market: False Start, Strong Follow-Through, and Now for the Finish' to *The State of the Economy* (IEA Readings No. 31, 1990).

Colin Robinson was educated at the University of Manchester, and then worked for 11 years as a business economist before being appointed in 1968 to the chair of Economics in the University of Surrey. He has been a member of the Electricity Supply Research Council and of the Secretary of State for Energy's Advisory Council for Research and Development in Fuel and Power (ACORD), and is currently on the electricity panel of the Monopolies and Mergers Commission. Professor Robinson has written widely on energy, including *A Policy for Fuel?* (IEA Occasional Paper No. 31, 1969); *Competition for Fuel* (Supplement to Occasional Paper No. 31, 1971); *The Energy 'Crisis' and British Coal* (IEA Hobart Paper No. 59, 1974); (with Jon R. Morgan), *North Sea Oil in the Future* (1978); (with Eileen Marshall) *What Future for British Coal?* (IEA Hobart Paper No. 89, 1981), and *Can Coal Be Saved?* (IEA Hobart Paper No. 105, 1985); and he contributed a paper, 'Privatising the Energy Industries', to *Privatisation & Competition* (IEA Hobart Paperback No. 28, 1989).

Professor Robinson became a member of the IEA's Advisory Council in 1982 and was recently appointed its Editorial Director.

Peter J. Warburton: After finishing graduate studies at Warwick University in 1975, Mr Warburton worked in the Centre for Economic Forecasting at the London Business School until 1981. He then moved to the City University Business School, combining economic research with lecturing responsibilities in economics and statistics. In 1986 he joined the stockbroker L. Messel & Co. (now Lehman Brothers) as an economist, where he developed a detailed UK forecasting model. Mr Warburton gained a PhD in 1988 based on published academic work. In January 1989 he joined Robert Fleming Securities as UK economist, publishing regular bulletins on economic and financial matters.

Mr Warburton's academic publications in economic forecasting, exchange rates and the UK labour market include articles in *Oxford Economic Papers, Explorations in Economic History* and the *Journal of Economic Affairs*; and contributions to *Economic Modelling* (ed. P. Ormerod, 1979); *The Money Supply and Exchange Rate* (ed. W. Eltis and P. Sinclair, 1981); *Work, Welfare and Taxation* (M. Beenstock *et al.*, 1987); and *Modelling the Labour Market* (ed. M. Beenstock, 1988).

Geoffrey E. Wood is Professor of Economics at the City University Business School. He has taught at Warwick University and been on the research staff of both the Bank of England and the Federal Reserve Bank of St. Louis. He is co-author of *Financing Procedures in British Foreign Trade* (1980), and co-editor of, among others, *Monetary Targets* (1980), *Financial Crises and the World Banking System* (1985), and *Macro-Economic Policy and Economic Interdependence* (1989). He is Economic Adviser to The Union Discount Company of London.

Professor Wood has been a member of the IEA's Advisory Council since 1987, and has recently (1991) been made a Trustee. For the IEA he has written (with Gordon Pepper) *Too Much Money . . .?* (Hobart Paper No. 68, 1976), and has contributed to other IEA Papers, including a Commentary in *The State of Taxation* (IEA Readings No. 16, 1977), and papers in *Could Do Better* (Occasional Paper No. 62, 1982), *Agenda for Social Democracy* (Hobart Paperback No. 15, 1983), and *Whose Europe?* (IEA Readings No. 29, 1989); he contributed a new Introduction to the Third Edition of F. A. Hayek's *Denationalisation of Money* (Hobart Paper No. 70, 1990); and he wrote the Introduction to *The State of the Economy 1991* (IEA Readings No. 34, 1991).